Introducti

They were both from California. He wrote ior the campus
paper with biting sarcasm and razor sharp wit and said whatever
the hell came to mind - with no apologies. She was a timid, naïve
girl who had the biggest music collection I'd seen and went buck
wild her freshman year after leaving home for the first time.

They've come a long way.

My experiences with both authors have been as roommates, coworkers, and friends. However, the relationships started out on
totally different footing. One became a close friend, the other
I couldn't stand the first time I met him. He's grown on me
since... :-)

Dara Shifrer

Student, researcher, music maniac, OCD journaler (or was once
upon a time), happy hour lover, world traveler, wine enthusiast,
free spirit, and music festival schedule color-coder extraordinaire
(you know you've arrived when your friends check with you for
show information instead of the official festival website). Oh,
and an amazing cook. Just check out her chow-chows one day if
you're that lucky.

I think my first bonding moment with Dara was in the college
dorm one day, discussing music. It was some ridiculous freestyle
album I had - I cringe today to think I even considered it good
stuff. I cringe that she **also** thought it was good stuff. The girl

had a music collection that rivaled a record shop - I was pretty impressed.

She also had a certain attraction for a bit of mischief.

Dara loves to push buttons and get people riled up. However, one day after mouthing off to her crush's roommate, she got thrown into the tiny dorm bathroom, with no way out.

(Constant banging and yelling persists for a few minutes).

"You gonna be nice and behave Dara?"

"Yesssss, let me out!!!"

The door opens, and there is shaving cream squirted everywhere as writing on the bathroom wall and so back in she goes (or gets pushed in) and they lock her up again for her punishment.

"You ain't comin' out until that's cleaned up!"

Meanwhile a group of us are in the room, pissing our pants laughing. Hell, even the RA found it hilarious and wouldn't help her. She finally got out about 10 minutes later...

Andrew Marx

Writer, web developer, music maniac, OCD budgeter (but his finances are in way better shape right now than mine, so who am I to judge?), restaurant lover, world traveler, great debater and proud owner of shapely calf muscles. Or so he had last I saw him

Praise for *What Do You Say to the DJ?*

"Too good! I already had a few laugh out loud bursts last night when I was reading, so you must have done something right."
-Gabrielle Harder

* * *

"*What Do You Say to the DJ?* is a laugh-out loud book that is both witty and well-written. The authors have no shame revealing the personal (almost too personal) details of their chaotically confusing lives. The book is a unique blend of story-telling intertwined with concert reviews of various bands."
-Kristina Reilly

* * *

"There are parts of this book that are pee-in-your-pants funny. I started reading, and immediately related to the characters. It's nice to know I'm not the only crazy person out there!! :-)"
-Chris Holsten

* * *

"It's really intriguing to find a story told in large part through the dominant medium of generations X and Y - email chains. And for as much as it's hard to imagine following a story that way, they pull it off. And along the way, Marx and Shifrer certainly have a way with turning phrases and telling micro stories that shape a developing image of a larger life, viewed only through clever snippets of the way life is for friends post-college: finding 10 minutes to finally respond to that last email."

-Jonathan Epstein

* * *

"…a rambling conversation about trying and being. you will like this. if not, then you are likely repressing quite a bit; that or you have found pure bliss and happiness. can you tell which??"

-Jeffrey Scott

* * *

"It's hard to figure out what's going on.

But, that's cool."

-Gary Marx

What Do You Say to the DJ?

EXPANDED EDITION

....

ANDREW MARX
AND DARA SHIFRER

Interior art by Tabitha Worthington

Cover photography by Mark Khan

ISBN: 1-4392-5718-3
ISBN-13: 9781439257180

Visit www.booksurge.com to order additional copies.

in shorts at a waterfront concert in Boston (Look Heather! I'm so proud of these, got them from busting my ass on the treadmill! Woo hoo!) He's intensely interesting, and probably the host of the most fun Trivial Pursuit game I ever played, complete with booze on a hot, late summer evening in Boston. However, Andrew is not for the weak. He's brilliant, he's hysterical, and he's brutally honest. If you ask for his opinion, brace yourself and make sure you want it. Likely he will tell you what you need to hear - not want to hear, and he's usually spot on after a bit of reflection.

He's even been accused of being insensitive in the past on occasion.

(Roommate's incessant, constant analyzing of doomed-from-the-start relationship that lasted four days, meanwhile analyzing went on for what seemed like four years):

"He said this, he did that, why why why???"

Andrew: "Um, seriously? You REALLY need to get over it at this point. It's been years and it's not gonna happen."

"You're hurting my feelings!"

And so... due to that exchange, no speaking and tension in the apartment for about a month. Yeah right. I'll take his side on this one... even 12 years later.

So, to you guys out there contemplating buying the book while reading this: buy the book. You can probably relate to most of the situations in the story. There's lots of funny stuff in here. Andrew and Dara have grown up for the most part since the shaving cream fights and insults of love unrequited. Sometimes they still have their days (*cough cough*) but buy the book because if you don't, you have no soul.

April 17, 2009

HEY, REPUBLIC

I'm engaged and need to send you an invitation immediately!

Ooh, fun. I'm giving birth to a Honda next week.

Chapter One *Hey Republic!*

---- Original Message ----
From: Andrew Marx
To: dshifrer
Subject: We'll Find a Way
Date: Sun, 6 Feb 2005

Okay, so I switched my website and e-mail over to a new host and so everything was lost, including whatever your last e-mail to me was. I thought I had backed up some of those files, but I guess not.

So anyway, I don't really have any idea if we were following a string of thoughts or particular conversation. I hear Julianna was with you in Austin during the New Year. I don't think I knew that. I had forgotten that she had called me some time ago and so I never called her back.

Today is Super Bowl Sunday and of course, that means Boston will be riotous. Probably whether the Patriots win or lose, Boston will be riotous. I have a friend from high school who is staying in town this week at a hotel downtown and I have one mission.

To somehow get her to her hotel in one piece, be it riot or traffic or Big Dig leaks.

Okay well this wasn't a "content" e-mail so much as a "welcome to my new e-mail address" except that my e-mail address is the same.

Confusion reigns,

Andy

From: Dara Shifrer
To: amarx
Subject: RE: We'll Find a Way
Date: Wed, 9 Feb 2005

I can't believe you lost my e-mail. I have no idea what it said either, but am positive that it was of import. And nothing happened in Boston after the Super Bowl, and the newscasters were far too blatant in their disappointment.

Who is this friend visiting? When are you going to Britain? I might be going to Belize for my Spring Break.

I am tired today. You know that I love to download. So, I am very distressed ever since I lost Kazaa and haven't found a good replacement. I am fiddling around with WinMX right now. My music knowness will vaporize if I don't find something soon. I really really loved it. And I referred one student (hate the final steps of discipline) and then put the final touch on the kicking out of another student from the school. It drains me, but I did both in eerie calmness, which is a good sign. Actions taken during rage haze are suspect. I am off to my GRE training meeting - my friend used to work for The Princeton Review - we are both having a really good time with it. Food is involved. Julianna did come to Austin for New Year's - she wore me out (ah, that was what my last e-mail was about...note, Andy, that was one month ago...tardy boy). What've you been doing lately outside of work and websites?

Dara

From: Andrew Marx
To: dshifrer
Subject: RE: We'll Find a Way
Date: Fri, 11 Feb 2005

I didn't lose your e-mail, it got deleted along with everything else on the server when I made the switch. There was a way to download the e-mails, but I opted not to because it didn't seem practical to save every e-mail that I have accumulated since college. I don't really remember anything about Julianna being mentioned anyway. I spoke to her this week. She told me she got a...how did she put it? A grown-up, salaried jobby-job. A real one. I would have told her a place in the workforce is overrated, that our college years were largely wasted worrying about "what lies ahead" but she'll figure it out soon enough. I expect we'll speak again in another six months or so.

The Super Bowl all around was not an exciting event for me. The Eagles played sloppy football and I was watching it with my roommate and his girlfriend who talked non-stop the entire time. Then, in the third quarter, she asked me, "Do you mind that we talk over the TV?" Um, why yes. Yes, I do. They did go to the grocery store and come back with a mighty spread of food. Wings, chips, salsa, beer. There is a means of redemption in there somewhere.

This is the same roommate that I play GameCube with a few nights a week. I think he has friends, but he spends most of the nights at home, at least so far. There are four of us in the house total. This one is adorable. Like Punky Brewster adorable. I think the other guys ignore him completely so to him, I'm the nice one. Imagine that.

I have a cd I made for you, but I wasn't sure if you wanted yet another mix. Its theme: Music I listened to the day I made it. So it's a combination of things, not all of them a surprise to you and some savory (and one that is directly from your collection). If you want it, I'll send it after I get back from London to visit my sister. It's got the track list printed on the cd face so you can't say I didn't include the song titles and artists.

The London trip will be pretty lowkey, my sister is skittish about spending money being underemployed and all. My mom will also be there for a couple of days at the same time I'm there. Most of my spare time now is spent thinking about preparing for the trip, trying to figure out all the logistics involved in this process. It's not really the distance that does it, it's the amount of time I'm going to be gone. From start to finish, I think it's eight

and a half days. The weird thing is that February is so com-
pressed that I get paid the day before I leave and I get paid the
day after I come back, not having worked a full day in between.
(Those kind of details make me giggle irrepressibly).

I am now near the end of my work day and my brain is in a
strange overcaffeinated tizzy.

Andy

From: Dara Shifrer
To: amarx
Subject: RE: We'll Find a Way
Date: Sun, 13 Feb 2005

Okay, of course, I want the compilation. I might bitch about
particulars but anyone willing to share music is all right by me.
You're the sort who I can bitch to in the expectation that you
will understand. You always introduce me to music I wouldn't
otherwise hear which is saying a lot. And by the way, I listened
to the Northern State CD you gave me (I think it's one you
don't personally listen to?) and I really enjoy it. They're funny
but satisfying. Female rap - totally reminiscent of that Bunny &
Tigre song "We like the cars - the cars that go boom." I doubt
you even know what I'm referencing, but maybe you do.

I was struck with the feeling today that every year of my life and
every day of my life brings something fantastic. Like I am totally
satisfied with the small events of my life. Even if I don't feel it

everyday or cast negativity on it, drama, it's always interesting. So glad I left Las Vegas.

Caffeine mania was mine today too. Unpleasantly. It's faded now, but there's a tired mania in effect. I booked a ticket to Belize this morning to visit the archaeologist I dated for a month. I am fearful on all counts, further cementing with him, visiting a jungle, etc. But I'm excited too.

Punky Brewster adorable is very attractive. He is girlfriended though? Your collection of friends is always intriguing. There seems to be great variety.

I haven't heard from your sister lately. I'm glad you're visiting. I expect a full account of the life of the girl-who-moved-to-Britian-for-a-guy-she-knew-4-months. Tell her that she was referenced in my teacher friend's English class. The writing prompt was "people who do grand things for love" and my friend told her story to motivate the class.

Dara

From: Andrew Marx
To: dshifrer
Subject: Hey Republic!
Date: Tue, 22 Feb 2005

I can't find the disc I made, but when I run across it again, I will send it to you. If not, I can always make you a new one. My big fav new sound right now is Bright Eyes (I know, I'm getting on the Wagon along with everyone else) but I like his folk-oriented tunes rather than the vague techno-blah that he put out on his new album. If you don't know Bright Eyes at all, then I'll include it on the next mix just because it lights up my life.

Okay, so no London. My outbound flight was delayed to begin with. They started to board but discovered some sort of mechanical abnormality and delayed the flight two hours (by this point, I would have already missed my connection to London) and then they cancelled the flight altogether. The airline was willing to rebook me, but the scenarios I was offered sucked kaka so I took a full refund and went home. My mom said later that I should have just sucked it up and gone with whatever they were willing to give me, but I was pretty okay with my decision. I did stay up Sunday night until 5am so I could call Megan and explain to her the situation.

She was disappointed (she booked a trip to Greece instead of hanging out with me) and my mom chastised me lightly for not rebooking. They both just wanted me there over the weekend to be interference for their mutual interactions since they rapidly tired of each other. I guess my mom wanted to do more tourist stuff and my sister wouldn't play the knowledgeable tour guide. In that respect, I would have been a useful addition because I do know my way around (I can read an Underground map at least) and I like to do the tourist trap stuff. I think my mom won't go back unless she takes someone with her (probably her boyfriend, who will spend money on her) to do those things.

It is weird these days with my sister. We don't have that easy flow of communication anymore. I'm not sure if it's the distance, or that nothing goes on in her world, or that nothing goes on in my world. I'm tired of worrying about the price of international calling, so I added a package to my cell phone so I can dial direct from anywhere in the states. It just gives me an easy way to deal, and now all I have to think about is the time difference. Although instead of staying up until 5am, I guess I could just get up at 5am which is only about 40 minutes earlier than my usual. Why that didn't occur to me earlier, I cannot say.

Anyhoo, I had a pretty productive weekend, just organizing my world, and my roommates and I have settled (almost) into a status quo. One of the roommates is kind of a slob about his dinners and cleaning up in the kitchen, but not putting the leftover pizza away for a couple days grosses me out on more of a bacterial invasion level than worrying about a) mice or ants b) stale pizza. I have duly tried to not be critical about everything and sort of loose and fun around the house and alternately invisible as much as possible.

Finally, work has been insane with almost full-moon-like hysteria that has invaded my office. I don't know if I mentioned it before, but my office space has turned into a sitcom. We have "adopted" some extra staff who were kicked out of another building and it's become a circus of personalities. Anyway, going with the theme of the week ("What are you doing here?") I have decided to avoid everyone more or less and play the invisible card.

By way of my mother, I can report that Megan is happy, settling in with her new boyfriend. My mom approves of the relationship, predicts that if they make it through the first year or so (particularly with Megan finding employment or fulfilling hobby) she probably won't come back to the states. I think that's cool. She did find some kind of work there, but whether it's a long term prospect or not, I don't think she really knows.

How's the world, Southern Belle? I asked Julianna if she wanted to chill in Providence this weekend, so I'm waiting to hear if she's around.

Andrew

From: Dara Shifrer
To: amarx
Subject: RE: Hey Republic!
Date: Thu, 24 Feb 2005

What wagon!?! Did I miss it!?! Believe me - don't beat yourself up over being one in a million in the Bright Eyes fanbase - the swelling of the fan base is not apparent here in Austin. Yeah, so I guess you ought to include it on the next compilation...esp if your life is being lighted. I've heard of them, but discarded as emo crap.

I am shocked at the London flight situation. I didn't think such things happened. I guess I don't often fly to exciting places. And how are you such an Underground expert? Who did you go with?

So did you move somewhere new? Only because you speak of your living situation as if it is new. I dread the thought of having to move b/c of problems in previous e-mail and having to find roommates. I am curious how you find your homes/roommates. And how you coexist, play music, walk nude.

Sara, Megan's old neighbor here, who is in Greece for this semester, also reports that your sister is happy. In regards to your communication problems, she stopped e-mailing me about one month ago. I was almost scared I had offended her, but then she sent me a mass e-mail and I suppose she is just really busy? As far as you, I suppose she is in a weird position - her life is so dramatically altered. Long-long-distance doesn't have that comfort level that within the states calls do.

So...you still like your job? You're not leaving Boston it seems like?

From: Dara Shifrer
To: amarx
Subject: RE: Hey Republic!
Date: Sat, 26 Feb 2005

Andy,

This is not my reply, but while I'm thinking on it, I've been running across a lot of your music lately. And James is such a great band. I've had their album forever and just listened to "Laid" like a mad woman (that song runs through my head on a daily basis), but all of a sudden last week I realized I love the whole album. Corey Byrne sounds like the lead singer of Live, but don't respond, because I feel like I asked about him before and you sent me a long response that I've forgotten.

From: Andrew Marx
To: dshifrer
Subject: RE: Hey Republic!
Date: Sun, 27 Feb 2005

I have also rediscovered the Laid album in the last month or so. I have really invested time in just going back over my collection and really just delving into the discs I ignore most of the time. It's not every moment of perfection, but it certainly has its highlights.

My brain is crazy at the moment. Work is busy and my homelife is shit and I can't escape my themes. You know all about the themes. I have perpetuated and masturbated them into a fugue state (the very definition of repetition, look it up!) Anyway, I had this funny notion that recently (last two months) I have been "laying the foundation" of my transition to the next phase of my life (you are already there, right?) But what's humorous about that is, what have I been doing for the last five years? Don't answer that. I know, I have been "TALKING" about laying the foundation for my new life.

So I am officially tired of the following topics:

dysmorphia
living paycheck to paycheck
winter (I am highly amused by it myself, but the naysayers are many and vocal)
anything related to or coming from my father
roommates

This whole e-mail put me in a wonderful mood. I've been brooding all day. I have this weird zen religious experience at the gym now, most times that I go. It's the only time I don't think about anything but breathing and sweating. For about 30 minutes each day my problems don't exist.

Anyway, as I'm sure Julianna has somehow already communicated to you, we had lunch. It was extremely pleasant and leisurely.

On with the show...

---- Original Message ----
From: Andrew Marx
To: dshifrer
Subject: Concert Site
Date: Wed, 21 Feb 2007

Can you look this over for my new website? It's a list of all of the concert categories I could think of. So I (not so arbitrarily) picked the primary category (listed first) and then the sub categories (same row). You can add any categories, rearrange subcategories or primaries. Just send me whatever you think is best so I can work it into the new site.

Category / Subcategories

1. Rock Hard Rock Alternative Rock Classic Rock Techno Rock Surf Rock New Wave Grunge
2. Classical
3. Theater Musical Opera Ballet Plays
4. Comedy
5. Latin
6. Country
7. Folk Bluegrass
8. Jazz Big Band
9. Blues
10. Metal
11. New Age Celtic Spoken Word
12. Dance Techno Ambient Trance Rave
13. Pop
14. Hip Hop Rap
15. R&B Soul Gospel Funk

16. Other World Music Holiday Christian Spoken Word Reggae Ska
17. Children Zydeco Middle Eastern Jewish
18. DJ Shows

From: Dara Shifrer
To: amarx
Subject: RE: Concert Site
Date: Fri, 23 Feb 2007

It looks great, Andy. You're lacking a Punk category though - and Reggae and Ska would do better under that category anyway. I'm sure pop could fit with something else - maybe make two rock categories - one with light rock categories (including pop) and one with hard rock categories (including punk). You could also throw hip-hop and rap in with the R&B category. Put DJ in with the dance category ... or the hip-hop/rap category. Category 17 is a little bizarre, but makes me want you to add Gypsy - it's the new It Genre. This is already Too Much fun. I almost pulled out my rock bible, but it's at Michael's house. I just might send you a more detailed analysis of this very important situation.

2

Chapter Two *To Punish Me For My Contempt For Authority, Fate Made Me An Authority Myself*

---- Original Message ----
From: Dara Shifrer
To: amarx
Subject: oh my god the o button
Date: Thu, 3 Mar 2005

I'm in no condition to write you, but if I wait until I am, then I'll never write. I have spent every evening this week utterly exhausted and mindless. I fully blame teaching. If you suddenly see the alf;jeawoinfviao of my head hitting the keyboard, you'll understand. It made me happy that you have "really invested time" into "really just delving" into your old CDs - you are at your most serious and dedicated when you speak of music. Which is why, only partly, I adore you.

All right, here's my themes. Totally overwhelmed. And it's my fault. Overwhelmed in the ST and LT of my life. Have so much planned and/or going on that it's wiping me out mentally and financially, but can't imagine living any other way. Besides these typical concerns, I have had a sore tongue intermittently (this word occurs because it was applied to my computer problem today) for months now, and it's really bothersome, but moreso because I can't figure the why of it out. And yesterday morning, I awoke to a leaky ceiling, and then yesterday evening came home to find my wall-rat (previously) rustling in my kitchen cupboard. The only trap I had was this save-the-rodent sticky surface one, and the thought of a stuck squealing rodent was so repellant that I slammed the cupboard door and walked away to let it be a silent scurrying rodent. And I've had a horrible week with the children - the weather turned sunny for a few days and they are all mad. Mad. If I stop for a second, which I don't, and look at them, it's funny because every single one of the 30-odd kids is doing some bizarre thing in one single moment. It's so not funny when I'm trying to accomplish something. And I blame it all on me, which makes it worse.

so okay what is this "next phase" that I have moved into. I don't see that. And maybe you're too defining with your life - these "phases" you perceive (I do the same thing). Life is a flow. That's the one pleasant part of my current life - I feel like it's suddenly totally out of my control and it's just a relief to throw up my hands. Take it! Do with it what you will! I've tried! But then you say Boston is developing nicely. Something more must be going on - you speak in grandeur without specific - here's what I've observed: you've been a little bit inconspicuous of late which leads me to believe that...something more has been going on. Why is the homelife shit?

Dysmorphia! So weird that you say that! The only other person I've heard use it was my boss at the temp agency here in Austin (a gay man), and he was a self-admitted victim of it. But, BUT, and god I hated him for it, his own insecurities resulted in criticism of me. He's the guy who sent me home for a wrinkled shirt one day (I'd ironed it but had bent it in the sitting while driving position), regularly commented on my outfits and my choice of hair wear. Guaranteed I was fresh from the Las Vegas warehouse and as clueless as always insofar as dress codes...you know what? I change my mind, I hated him hard forever, but his insanity forced me to resign and give in to professional wear. I am so much more conscious now. Spend money on it now.

Gym zen is good. I feel it too, even if I know it's a little perverse and ill all the while. I'm trying to up the gymness currently. Sometimes I feel extremely bothered to be apart of these people who spend a good chunk of time each day facing in one direction on machines that have no function and go no where. It's strange. And you know it. It sounds like you go every day.

I did not know that you saw Julianna...and you imagined that we speak of nothing much but you! Ha! Actually I haven't spoken to her lately.

To bed,

Dara

From: Andrew Marx
To: dshifrer
Subject: Ringtones as an Income Stream
Date: Wed, 16 Mar 2005

Spring fever has hit big time. It's just sunny enough to entice and just cold enough to keep wearing those jackets and gloves. My car is wheezing through its final winter, it barely starts on the first try any more and there's something underneath that rattles furiously when you brake. Is that what old age is like? I want to put him down, but I sorta figure I'll wait until he hits the senior wall and then plug him with diesel.

It makes me sad on the one hand (first car I've ever owned) and jubilant on another (piece of crap mounted on wheels/no excuse not to replace). The parts have wicked value though. One mechanic offered to buy the car from me even if it stops running. I probably should have sold it when he offered but I had just put three hundred dollars into passing state inspection and damnit, I'm going to get my three hundred dollars back in use.

I'm leaving for Vegas on Friday for a six day trip including a four day conference at MGM Grand. A few of my colleagues will be there but I have the first part of the weekend to myself. I'm really looking forward to being away, and of course, it's some reimbursable expenses. Hard to fault that. I'm on a non-stop flight. Six hours on a plane. Yikes, but I kick ass at the music trivia (you play against other travelers).

At the moment it's 4pm and my attention span has just sputtered out. I should probably go home, but I don't want to miss anything.

From: Dara Shifrer
To: amarx
Subject: RE: Ringtones as an Income Stream
Date: Mon, 21 Mar 2005

I got swiped in traffic. I pulled into a lane and a big brown van pulled in seconds later and bruised my right front bumper. He got out, smiled at me, surveyed the damage and jumped back in. I assumed since we were both capable of moving that we were heading out of the traffic, but after following him for ten minutes, I started feeling the fuel and gave up my fantasy. It was a hit-and-run, friendly style. I filed a police report. I don't want the man in prison, but I would like my insurance deductible paid.

Happy discovery is, the left front bumper has been damaged (my fault) since Week 1 with the car, and now we have a chance for all bumpers to be fixed. But it's a pain in the ass of paperwork and deductibles and whatnot. I don't have the stomach for it until Thursday frankly.

I am aglow with the wonders of good travel and a better man. This attitude is enabled by my recent return from Belize. It was wonderful.

I saw the city, the mountains and the beach. Rode horses, snorkeled, and flew in a four-seater plane. And was romanced like I never have been in my life.

I heard that you're going to Las Vegas. From Julianna of course. She says you're going with Becca too? What business takes you there? I suspect you'll be gambling there. Belize had a casino so similar to a Vegas casino it was eerie. The city was dreggy but the casino was not. I did pretty fine on blackjack.

Your car deserves much respect. If it's the car I remember - it's, sorry, been a piece of shit for quite some time. How have you done it? You must be a superior maintainer. Or you don't wreck cars at the pace that I do. I am unmatched in my wrecking ability.

You looove your job now.

Dara

From: Andrew Marx
To: dshifrer
Subject: RE: Ringtones as an Income Stream
Date: Sat, 26 Mar 2005

I wasn't aware that Becca and I were going to Las Vegas. I actually just got back from Vegas. It was pleasant. Not great, not epiphanal, just pleasant. Spent the weekend strolling up and down the Strip with my mother. The Fashion Show Mall has blossomed into a full scale high end shopping arena. It's visually stunning and has a ton of stores (although now they can justify the prices). We also spent some time at Aladdin and at Mandalay Bay and the Tropicana. It was a lot of walking in the wrong shoes and many quarters plucked into machines. Not a lot of winning going on but we managed to stretch our playtime out each day.

The trip was work too, and I spent most of my waking hours weaving through crowds of people that were in Vegas to gamble, while I learned about trends in higher education technology. I picked up some interesting tidbits for my job.

On to cars: I don't get into accidents. I just never did. One time, a kid hit me (he had had his license for a week) in the parking lot at school and he was going down the wrong direction of a one-way lane. It happened in front of the principal! Another time, the woman stopped in the middle of the road and I hit her from behind. (Both in the same year). I would also argue that wasn't my fault, but I was too young to figure out what to do to avoid hitting her.

I think cars are way dangerous and drivers are fucking scary, so I do my diligence and it seems to work for me. I have only gotten one speeding ticket in my life, driving to Texas nonetheless, and the cop inflated my speed in order to meet the minimum for writing the ticket because he knew I wouldn't come back to fight it in the middle of nowhere, Texas. He also roughed me up as if I was drug dealer, which I find highly dubious. I imagine you heard that story before because we drove through that same spot the next year.

I don't know where Belize is, or that you would be there. I haven't romanced in a while, but I finally had a great, jovial evening of fits of laughter while visiting with some of my old coworkers from UNLV. Why isn't life like that anyway? I don't know, it seems sad that we don't more often have freedom to just find everything ridiculously amusing. When I get back to Boston, I develop this simultaneous sense of belonging and cranked anxiety. It seems self-defeating.

You and I should travel together again. Would it be worth it? I'm not sure where we could go but I have a good U.S.-based list of my own, plus some more ambitious foreign travel that I can't really afford.

Signing off,

Andrew

From: Dara Shifrer
To: amarx
Subject: RE: Ringtones as an Income Stream
Date: Wed, 30 Mar 2005

Since when does one expect Vegas to be great, epiphanal or pleasant? Certainly not this girl. I thought that you had developed an enormous hate for Vegas - never to step foot there again? I don't where these rumors start...you sound reconciled to Vegas now. And please tell me why you wax so positive about the New England area? The people? The weather? The lifestyles? There's a definite undertone of positivity lacing your e-mails of late! Tell me the real gossip Andy.

Of course we should travel together! We've actually racked up a bit of traveling I just realized - LV to Austin and then New Orleans. I really enjoy driving with you - lots of conversation and music. Or do I hate battling over the music with you?... Did I tell you I'm going to Eastern/Central Europe in July? With said guy. It was my trip initially - to take advantage of newfound relatives in Slovenia - it has blossomed into a circle of countries in that area. Very very excited am I.

Bye!

Dara

From: Andrew Marx
To: dshifrer
Subject: After a year like this one, I'm surprised I'm not closer to God
Date: Tue, 5 Apr 2005

There isn't much in the way of news on my end. I guess Megan's getting married, but that's her news, not mine.

Remarking on your last e-mail:

Before I landed in Vegas, I felt like I was going home. Once I was there, I did not feel like I was home at all, but it was a pleasant experience. The land now seems very foreign to me overall and I guess I was just surprised to realize that. Maybe nothing's really changed that much but I wasn't feeling the connection.

As for never-stepping-foot-there-again, I think that is probably an unlikely outcome. Three times a year, that's more to the tune. Plus it's the cheapest place to fly to from Boston. Anything in that area, Phoenix/Los Angeles -cheap-o.

As for New England, I have a great fondness for the traditional values on display. I never knew where they originated, and certainly California isn't true to the Puritanical tradition. But here, people are all over that. Each season has its rituals. Behavior has a set standard and everyone has this transcendental awareness of the stereotypes and categorizations that accord with this ancient system of How Things Are. The seasons are really colorful here and I like that. I like that you can drive for six hours in any direction and cover four or five states. (I hardly ever remember that Boston harbors the Atlantic Ocean, but it's there to the east). New York State is ridiculously oversized. There are still a lot of small business-privately owned consumer shops here and so much of New England has history. History, I might add, that I am barely familiar with so any time I need an adventure, it's there.

The thing that amuses me most about this particular breed of humanity is that everything is a brand new concept. Any situation, any circumstance, any topic, people always act like they have never heard of it before. Snow comes out of the blue. Winning sports team is a foreign novelty. Losing sports teams is even more unheard of. Government corruption in the news and people scratch their heads like "people really do that?" There is no precedent for anything, the DNC, terrorist threats, highway maintenance, a pedestrian run over by a commuter train, the melting of the Charles River, the freezing of the Charles River, the Boston Marathon, it's all brand new, like a Christmas present unwrapped. And this sort of reductive amnesia covers residents on 1,000 miles of New England coastline.

Slovenia sounds novel. How do you possibly plan a trip there?

Andy

26

From: Dara Shifrer
To: amarx
Subject: To punish me for my contempt for authority, fate made me an authority myself
Date: Tue, 5 Apr 2005

Andrew Marx!! What are you thinking!?! Just wait til I go and tell on you! Ruining the glorious fun of a surprise for me. Oh it will come back to you. It will. I wanted to unread it the second I'd read it, but I couldn't... How does it feel? How do you feel now that you have done such a thing!

So you feel....about this purported marriage? Is it a marriage for business or for love? Or is there a difference dear Andy? The business of life demands that love be conjured. I imagine that this is a motivation for her visit to Austin at the end of this month. And what am I supposed to do when Megan pulls this fabulous news out of her shoes? I will not pretend. I will not!

Very interesting summation of the northeastern parts - funny meld of daily life standards and no situational standards. You made it sound really unappealing to me. Like they're all ignoramus conservative naïve traditionalists. Maybe my interpretation. I do remember when I moved to Austin, and this is actually at Megan's house with you in attendance, and being appalled/ intrigued by the conversation at her party. People were so unironic and "genuine" about life pursuits - like marriage, babies, etc. It was striking to me, but I certainly don't notice that now, so have probably become one of them. Not that it's all bad, because the lack of that in Vegas was a lot of posturing, cool-consciousness and denial of basic human interactions.

Ooooh! A thunder storm just started. Lovely. Oh, now I feel bad. I read a review last night of a poet and he was totally condemned for his weather sentimentality. The critic would quote lines about the sweet rain and cute dew with such cutting disdain and I was sitting there thinking...but it is sweet and it is cute.

You know what I want to find Andy? A place without judgment or strife but still with challenge. A job I mean. Oh this is very of the moment. I got my annual review back and I was rated "average." How fucking horrible is that? It wouldn't have been so bad, because I'm not so much of a striving girl, but my principal was so apologetic about it, that I felt worse. I could give you all of the rationalizations (I got a far far better review last year...), but whatever. I thought of this because when I imagine the abuse that writers go through it is appalling. I don't know how they bear it. I am of the mind to say the teenage fuck-it, but I feel like I'm past that point, so then I could accept my criticism like a woman, but no...because it's just not fair! And then I'm a whiner. I was marked down for not having rapport with the students - please! I have too much. Which hurts my...ohh I'm talking about it. Never mind.

Planning Slovenia? Pshaw! It's not difficult at all! Books on ebay for under $5, obsessive hours at the computer, reading and taking notes, job done! The entire trip is planned. Planning trips is the light of my life frankly. I believe I have some 10 documents on the thing. Next time you and Megan need a trip planned... make sure you don't call me. ;-) You guys may have been uncooperative, but it certainly was a great trip.

Dara

---- Original Message ----
From: Megan Marx
To: undisclosed-recipients:;
Subject: here it is...
Date: Fri, April 1, 2005

The announcement:
Kevin and I are getting married. we are planning to have a private civil ceremony next month and a big bash reception around october-ish. it's obvious to us that we cannot get all of our loved ones in one place for the ceremony due to timing, previous commitments and money. and since it's very important to us that either everyone be there or no one be there, we are not including family in the ceremony. please, please do not feel slighted. we would much rather see everyone at a party, than a quiet ceremony and we cannot justify asking you all to drop everything to be there.

The plan:
The ceremony will be in vegas, as visa paperwork is easier if we marry outside the uk. we're planning to do this in the morning in the middle of the week and then proceed to l.a. to complete my (spouse) visa application and interview process. this can take anywhere between one day and 8 weeks to complete. if necessary, I will stay on to await my visa and kevin will return to england.

And finally:
Please believe that kevin and I have tried to consider all the details of our situation and everyone else's plans (the ones we're aware of). we feel best about this arrangement. we intend to announce our wedding to everyone else after the fact, as a save-the-date-for-the-reception kind of thing. since the visa process might

take some time, we would like to complete that before making a big announcement and beginning to plan our celebration.
talk to you soon..

Big squishy kisses,

Megan and Kevin

From: Andrew Marx
To: dshifrer
Subject: here it is...
Date: Tue, 5 Apr 2005 02:14:22

I honestly thought she had sent this to more people than just family, so I guess that was my mistake for thinking it was public knowledge. Well, I was never very good at holding things internally. When she asks how you found out, just say that I took out an advertisement in the Post.

Please note the time stamp on my e-mail. My roommate's poker game was relatively calm and quiet and for whatever reason after the guests had left (probably alcohol induced) at 1am, he started blaring music. It lasted about 1/2 an hour after which he promptly passed out and I am faced with a long night wide awake and a full day of work tomorrow. I'm making macaroni and cheese.

I'm in a wild state of irrationality so I kept my e-mail to him brief lest I unwittingly suggest where he can go shove it.

I also, much to my amusement, responded to work e-mails. Might as well be productive awake as I am.

From: Dara Shifrer
To: amarx
Subject: RE: here it is...
Date: Sat, 9 Apr 2005

I think it's hilarious that you sent an e-mail to your roommate to express your displeasure at his inappropriate behavior. I know exactly what kind of irrational mood you were
in - unwanted late nights put me in the same state. Lose all
perspective. What was his response to your e-mail? Really
hilarious Andy.

Strange thing happened. I got an unexpected package from you.
Stranger thing happened. It was an Erasure CD - I cocked my
head and thought - maybe a cruel joke? Note read: "Dear Jamie
[? - indiscernible a little], Concert souvenir..." So either package
contents were mixed up or I was never intended to receive anything. Please send me info on how to proceed - I would be happy
to forward on to proper recipient.

Are you excited for Megan? Or dismayed? I don't know why I ask
you questions like that - I think you hate them. Her e-mail was
interesting - very careful of people's feelings and reactions. I guess
family gatherings do require that of a person. Megan's the wise
sort who anticipates the fervor that weddings will undoubtedly
cause.

Write soon, bye,

Dara

From: Andrew Marx
To: dshifrer
Subject: RE: here it is...
Date: Sat, 9 Apr 2005

Your package went to my brother then, bummer. It was the guy at UPS who messed up, he put the stickers on the wrong packages (although I thought I watched him do it correctly, so it probably was something with how he input the addresses into the system).

I don't have any thoughts on a swap. Yours was a nicer package of discs, but it isn't worth shipping it back here, nor on to my brother.

If I get inspired about the packages, I'll let you know.

Andy

From: Dara Shifrer
To: amarx
Subject: RE: here it is...
Date: Sun, 10 Apr 2005

I am disappointed then! I would love to receive new music - I was thinking today how weary I am of my collection. I am still in a state of consuming music at a rapid rapid pace. It really would not be a big deal for me to throw the disc into the mail - send me your brother's address. The chances of me listening to an Erasure disc are infinitesimally slim - in fact, I would rather not have it disgrace my collection with its presence. ;-) If I recall correctly, Megan is a huge fan? I remember teasing her about them. Seems the whole family is!

I haven't had a lot of contact with her myself of late. She e-mails infrequently and without a lot of insight into her new life, but I just assumed that was her way. Well, it's a pretty unique situation. I couldn't tell from her e-mail if they are claiming to marry for love or for practicality. She was expressly against marriage before she left - well, I think a month or so prior she softened a tad. But still it didn't sound like it was her top option. Apparently close contact has changed that. I don't know...I'm of the school that believes that 75% of marriages, if not all, are entered into under faulty motivations.

OH! The person I am dating who does not live in Austin surprised and shocked me yesterday when he brought up...Suedomsa! Andy! Putting our old little selves on the internet for all to see. He googled my name and found it. In further discussion, I found out my sister has also seen it through that method. She said she liked it. I gave you all the credit. I haven't seen your website in a long time, speaking of. Send me the link again to remind me.

Bye! Dara

From: Andrew Marx
To: dshifrer
Subject: There Isn't A Man I Learned to Say No To
Date: Mon, 11 Apr 2005

Dara, I spent over a hundred bucks to see Tori Amos with a friend and it was highly, highly excellent. She played about 20 songs, and quite a few I had never heard live before, or just were songs I had never paid much attention to. I like that a lot because they were enjoyable and kind of new to me, even though some of the songs are 10 years old. She put on an exquisite performance. Her, two organs, the piano and the Rhodes. Her voice really came out because she wasn't drowned out by her band.

I also discovered a new performer that did a great opening show, but I'm still evaluating his studio prowess. As I have since found out from my brother that he is not sending you the studio disc I made for you (the live one is a companion disc to it that really isn't complete without the other - but I didn't tell my brother that because he was kind enough to offer to send the one to you) I'll make you a different one. The performer's name is Matt Nathanson. He's a wise-cracking singer. He covered the James song "Laid" on the American Wedding soundtrack. (I don't remember liking his version, but it's notable for his taste choice anyway).

I think secretly, my sister's marrying for love. But she doesn't want anyone to rain on her parade, so she's saying it's for practical purposes. She's giddy about it. Our family has a tradition of deflating hopes and dreams, so part of her isolationism is related directly to that.

Suedomsa is available in whole, though, at http://suedomsa.com/. That was the first thing I reposted when I switched webhosts.

Adios,

Andrew

From Concert-Central.com
Tori Amos, The Bushnell, Hartford, CT April 10, 2005
Review by Andrew

Tori Amos is one of those musicians that defies description and needs to be experienced. Not to say that everyone enjoys the ride, but you can't just up and answer the question, "Well, what kind of music does she play?" It's not that simple.

Her current tour has her supporting The Beekeeper with just herself and the various incarnations of pianos and organs that graced the stage. The stripped down versions of the songs were very faithful to the album versions. The result was a potent emphasis on her voice, that shown in songs like "Carbon" and "Jackie's Strength." Her best tunes of the night were focused on the piano, "Beauty Queen/Horses" and "Silent All These Years." Those sounded crisp in the auditorium and didn't drown out her vocals.

A theme of mourning and reflectiveness has pervaded her tour this time around. "The Beekeeper" ends the show, with homage to her deceased brother. It was a different mood for Tori and her fans, but she pulled it off exquisitely. "The Beekeeper" itself was a downer to the max, it sounded just like a church hymn ratcheted up on the decibels. Some people think the tune is beautiful (in my opinion, owing more to the theme than the melody) but to me, it was a woman working out some serious demons and it hurt.

Tori is paying special attention to cover songs on this tour, and tonight she pulled out two wholly unique choices. "59th Street

Bridge Song" was so remarkably upbeat that it contrasted sharply to the rest of the night. Same with a riveting cover of Janis Joplin's "Me and Bobby McGee." Her demeanor was so different during those two songs that it caused a sharp, and welcome, break in the somber mood.

From Concert-Central.com
Matt Nathanson, The Bushnell, Hartford, CT April 10, 2005
Review by Andrew

Matt Nathanson was a charming opening act. He opted for in between song banter that had the crowd laughing, and an energetic approach to his collection of songs. He played solo on one of two guitars and even tried to engage the audience in a singalong with lyrics that made no sense (he admitted as much to us). He was signing and selling cds after the show. I would have bought the cd, but waiting to get past the screaming young girls and gray-haired middle-aged gay men who wanted an autograph seemed like too much effort.

From: Dara Shifrer
To: amarx
Subject: RE: There Isn't A Man I Learned to Say No To
Date: Sat, 16 Apr 2005

I think that is the most shock I have heard you register...ever. You LOVE Tori!! LUOVUOUE her. I still count that show I saw with you as my favorite ever ever - I really like her but not like you louve her but at that show she was incredibly moving.

I think I near cried, I know I did, I'm sure I've told you this story.

I totally know what you mean in your sum-up of Megan. You both have that ironic downplay side to you. I think our generation has a habit of denigrating marriage once it comes - we spend our youth defaming it and can't own up to wanting it when we do. My best friend from high school, Sara, told me she was marrying my college friend Tom (you probably met him - oh what a clash of spirits you two would be - you must not have met him because I would remember it) because it was financially prudent. And I was annoyed and didn't attend the wedding back east when the invitations came. Years later, she is still upset with me for missing one of the most important events in her life, because, turns out, they were in love. Whatever. Oh! There is such a funny song called "Whatever." This guy depicts little scenes, you imagine him walking down city sidewalks, and then the music goes punkish and he says "Whatever!" no matter what the variation of situation. His name is Liam Lynch - the song is "United States of Whatever" or something. There has been a rash of Blue Man Group gifts to me lately. Gag.

Andy, I am writing-while-incoherent. So tired but unknowing of it, because of allergy medicine and coffee. AND my cat Crahobi is driving me MADDDDD! He keeps coming in and out just for the fun of it and I want to kick him. Hard. I am far too irritable to be awake.

Good night!

Dara

From Concert-Central.com
Stickpony, Hole in the Wall, Austin, TX April 16, 2005
Review by Dara

TheNewHippie's latest band, he described it as "cow punk," I'd describe it as crap. Funny sardonic lyrics, improved as set went on, loved it for the joy of seeing TheNewHippie on stage, I took pictures for him to send to father

From: Andrew Marx
To: dshifrer
Subject: Move South
Date: Mon, 25 Apr 2005

It turns out that my sister didn't plan on telling anyone officially until after the wedding, but what do I know? Have you talked to her? She's in Austin and I know she wants to meet up with you. You don't have to pretend to be ignorant, I confessed my goof. She's not, well it's not a tight lipped secret, she simply didn't want people to feel obligated to buy gifts or celebrate her union. Have you ever known my sister to be the secretive kind? My mom is ridiculously upset. I'm not the only good child left, but my competition is slipping.

Megan's pretty wrapped up in her fancy, and that's okay with me. I respect the fact that she is willing to do it the way that makes sense for her. I'm a big fan of making decisions that are in your own best interests. I think my mom respects that too, she just can't separate the rational approach from the emotional reaction.

On a related topic, I finally broke down and booked a ticket for my step-sister's wedding in August. I also sent her my tuxedo measurements, and no, I'm not in the wedding. It's not that I don't want to go (because I don't) but if I am going to take a stand with my father over our lack of familial relationship, that is not the hot-button issue I would choose to do it with. Ergo, I booked the ticket and probably will need to investigate hotel/rental car in the near future since that's the last weekend before Labor Day.

My brother says thank you, he loves the Erasure cd like another wife. I knew he would. I'm not insensitive to your musical tastes, but next time I'll have to mail the discs on different days. He said he mailed you something, but at this point, I don't remember what I put on it, just that it was all live tracks. Probably not very interesting (it was never meant to be separated from the studio disc).

Speaking of, I am making you a "Replacement Disc" which will be mailed next time I'm at the postal store. Probably beginning of next week. I like to be vague so that maybe it's still a surprise when it arrives. I'm thinking Matt Nathanson "Maid" and if I can get a hold of Elkland's new cd, I'll put "Apart" on there. The video is so funny. I actually have that, I wonder if I could copy it? If you didn't get the Buzz Gamble song (I think my brother kept that disc) I'll throw that on as well. Buzz died at the beginning of this year, so I'm memorializing him until 2006.

I'm deadset on moving out of my current situation which is pretty miserable for me. The new roommates are total slobs and everything is wet and smelly all around the house. The bathroom trash hasn't been emptied in ages and at this point, I refuse to do it. The bottom line is that I need to live in a house where I do not have to advise my guests to wear shoes in the kitchen.

Case in point, my roommate looks out the window and says wistfully, "What a dumb ass I am. I put that entertainment unit outside and now it's ruined." Um, yeah because it rained all weekend. Now he wants to find an axe to chop it up into pieces. So instead of a whole entertainment unit rotting in the back yard, we can have pieces of an entertainment unit rotting in the backyard.

Oh Dara, my car broke down officially and I sold it for parts (basically covered this year's repairs). I am gloriously freed, I can't explain it except Libertad! I walk to work most days (except heavy rain days - it just seems impractical) and it's wonderful. I discovered that the Trader Joe's that I shop at every month is actually only 10 minutes down the road (walking). I can get pretty far with just an hour of time. I can't explain why it's more liberating than having the car, but whatever. It just has really worked for me, at least until the temperature drops in October.

Alright, it's time to work and the coffee has sprung me loose!

Andy

From: Dara Shifrer
To: amarx
Subject: RE: Move South
Date: Mon, 2 May 2005

Well, that's not saying so much for your brother's wife. He returned my CD as well - very sweet of him. Soon I'll be interacting with your parents as well as all of your siblings.

I saw your sister this weekend finally. She was kind of bright and chipper but there was this strain of falseness about it - like she's nervous underneath. Maybe it's natural with all of the dramatic choices that she's making, but it does make me uncomfortable with her comfort level with her choices. Blah blah blah. She reported nothing but good. I think your sister IS secretive - well not secretive but definitely private - though not as private as yourself... She's not talking about the marriage as far as I know. It was good to see her. I am to eat pancakes on Saturday with her. She's a fun combination of silly and then sharp wit.

Congratulations on doing The Right Thing in regards to step sister wedding. You and weddings. This is the now theme of your life, right?

I'm all full of anxiety about my potential wedding. Not even. The guy I've been "dating" is in town from Belize for a month and we're adjusting to each other's nearness. It's great to have access to each other again, but he's a PhD student and has time to spend, and my time is regimented. I go to bed at 9pm... It's all of this stupid piddly stuff, but one of the reasons that his marriage didn't last is because his wife wanted him cleaning at

8am on Saturday mornings and he preferred 1pm (I think he preferred not but), and I understood his annoyance, marriage is rife with them, but I could see her point and/or where we'll have same differences And it just seems such a fat waste of energy, time and heartache to work at things that will inevitably end. That's pathetic. I like him so so much and it makes me anxious to actually care about how things are going between us. I think I was happier single. ;-) It's been an intense five days. We need separation but I can't seem to summon the willpower to make that happen.

Congratulations on the loss of the car! I'm surprised you don't miss it even a little. Maybe you do by now. How do you get to places that are far? How!?!

My glands are swollen today and my right wrist is very sore. I feel petulant and as if my life is unmanageable today. Because I need sleep and I need time to comb my f*&(*ing hair (school system won't send profane e-mails). My cat hates me. Guys don't understand the trials of being female. I will never get married. Mark my words Andy Marx. Never.

Ever.

Love, Dara

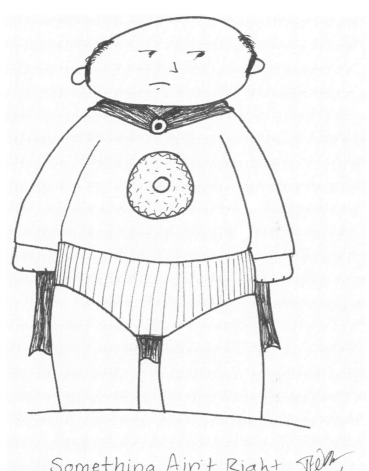

Something Ain't Right

10/08

---- Original Message ----
From: Dara Shifrer
To: amarx
Subject: RE: Concert Site
Date: Mon, 9 Apr 2007

I'm just going to send you my list of rock categories - I have to feel like i'm posting accurately. I'll do it today or tomorrow - as long as you don't mind! I have a thing for these subgenres. I think they're very nifty and they please my inner categorizer.

From: Dara Shifrer
To: amarx
Subject: RE: Concert Site
Date: Mon, 9 Apr 2007

Okay, attached is my obsessive genres list. I used the web to compile it - I don't walk around with this library in my head is what I mean. Do with it what you want. If it's too much, I can whittle several off, because I don't know what all of them mean. I just think that a list like this might move a music head to want to post because of the extensiveness of the genre list. This could be my own personal fantasy.

Classical music – Baroque, Chamber, Choral, Early Classical, Impressionist, Modern, Opera, Piano, Romantic, Symphony

Jazz – Dixieland, Swing, Big Band, Ragtime, Hard Bop, Cool Jazz, Free Jazz, Jazz Fusion, Smooth Jazz, Bebop, Acid Jazz, Avant Garde, Classic Jazz, Fusion, Latin Jazz

Blues – Acoustic Blues, Chicago Blues, Contemporary Blues, Country Blues, Delta Blues, Electric Blues, Cajun/Zydeco

Rhythm and Blues – Classic R&B, Funk, Contemporary R&B, Doo Wop, Motown, Neo-Soul, Quiet Storm, Soul, Urban Contemporary, Gospel

Soft Rock – Pop, Singer/Songwriter, Boy Band, New Age, Indie Pop, Noise Pop, Power Pop, Oldies, Adult Contemporary, Barbershop, Bubblegum Pop, Teen Pop

Rock – Psychedelic, Prog Rock, Hard Rock, Glam, Heavy Metal, Southern Rock, Roots Rock, British Invasion, Classic Rock, Garage Rock, Jam Bands, Rock & Roll, Rockabilly

Alternative Rock – Classic Alternative, College, Dancepunk, Dream Pop, Britpop, Goth, Emo, Grunge, Shoegazer, Indie Rock, Industrial, Modern Rock, Punk, New Wave, Post-Punk, Hardcore, Thrash, Cowpunk

Country – Honky Tonk, Bluegrass, Outlaw Country, Folk, Alt-Country, Americana, Classic Country, Contemporary Country, Contemporary Bluegrass, Western

Electronic/Dance – Acid House, Ambient, Big Beat, Breakbeat, Disco, Downtempo, Drum 'n' Bass, Electro, Garage, Hard House, House, IDM, Jungle, Progressive, Techno, Trance, Tribal, Trip Hop

Reggae – Ska, Dub, Rock Steady, Jam Band, Dancehall, Reggaeton, Contemporary Reggae, Ragga, Roots Reggae

Hip Hop/Rap – Alternative Rap, Dirty South, East Coast Rap, Freestyle, Gangsta Rap, Old School, Turntablism, Underground Hip-Hop, West Coast Rap

International – Latin American, African, Arabic, Asian, Brazilian, Caribbean, Celtic, European, Filipino, Greek, Hawaiian/Pacific, Hindi, Indian, Japanese, Jewish, Mediterranean, Middle Eastern, North American, Soca, South American, Tamil, Worldbeat, Zouk

From: Andrew Marx
To: dshifrer
Subject: RE: Concert Site
Date: Tue, 10 Apr 2007

Added Outlaw Country - but now you have to use it. What's Art Rock, is that sub of alt-rock?

3

Chapter Three *Something Ain't Right*

From Concert-Central.com
Flametrick Subs, Beerland, Austin, TX August 6, 2005
Review by Dara

They have an incessant numbers of gigs and after hearing them
at the roller derby I'd discounted them as some sort of wedding
singer group for the roller derby set but they had a shtick and did
it ever stick, 4 Satan's Cheerleaders, one stump-armed upright
bassist, a hard-drinking Irish guitarist, a standing-up female
drummer and a charismatic poetic ex-heroin-addict lead male
vocalist, lots of Cramps covers and same-old (as far as Austin
punk scene) rockabilly stuff but the lighting and the sparks of
everybody on the stage made it memorable

---- Original Message ----
From: Andrew Marx
To: dshifrer
Subject: I Was There When It Rang
Date: Wed, 31 Aug 2005

Dara,

I had the best dessert last night; creme brulee cheesecake. It was so awesome, I OD on sugar afterwards, and the scale refused to accept my new weight.

I received your birthday mailing. Thank you. It's nice to know you're still in the universe; it's been so long. I hear vague things from Julianna about you that have no rhyme or reason. She has made friends with friends of mine in Boston, so when I won't answer my phone, she calls them instead.

I spent last week in Portland, Oregon with Megan and Kevin. Got to know him a little more. Extremely nice chap. Just really enjoyed his company. It was a pleasant week - a lot more drinking than my usual. My aunt and uncle and grandmother live up in Portland so we did some family time and ate well. I had my first Americano at a place called Stumptown. The guy behind the counter asked me if an Americano was okay, but having never heard of it, I had no idea what I was being served. When he handed my aunt and I two cups of boiling water, we both burst out laughing.

The guy offered me two shots for it, I guess to entice me into thinking I was drinking actual coffee. Once he poured the first shot of espresso, it made more sense but the result was not a particularly exciting cup of coffee. My aunt was far less pleased than I, but I made the best of my first Americano with a generous serving of sugar and creamer.

Then last weekend, my step-sister got married, so we all journeyed to San Diego. The wedding ceremony was very nicely done, very tasteful. The chupah was decorated with tea lights that represented deceased family members, and also various other flowers and vines. They had white rose petals scattered down the aisle. The ceremony was very short and touching. Drinks before dinner were outdoors and the reception itself was inside.

The best story from the weekend - and I'll be the first to admit it was a nicer wedding (and weekend) than I would have expected - was driving with my father to get a manicure. My father invited his three boys to go with him and being the attentive, loving sons we are, we said yes. On the way there, my father asked my nineteen year old brother if he had gotten laid yet and went so far as to imply that he could use a good boning. From the back seat, I asked my dad, "Why didn't you ever have that talk with me?" His idea of a sex talk was to pass along a mega-sized box of condoms that I never got around to using before they expired - I didn't know what to do with one, much less two hundred.

My father's reply was classic. He said, "Because you never seemed interested. I would say 'look at her' and you would be looking" in any other direction except that he didn't say the words *in any other direction* but actually did this wave of his head as he was driving, of a person trying to look anywhere but towards what was being pointed out. My brother, the older one, and I burst out laughing because it was so true, and so me. My father then said, "I asked you what your type was, but you never responded." We busted up in the backseat.

Oh Dara, getting a manicure was disgusting. The place smelled acrid, and the women looked at us like aliens. She took a cuticle clipper and started stabbing away at my skin around the nail, ripping off little bits that collected under the point of the clipper in a wet glop. The buffing just hurt, and I missed the point of the clear coat of nail polish. It started peeling a day later in small strips.

A guy who works for me advised me not to repeat this story because, well you know it makes me seem like a girl.

AM

From Concert-Central.com
The Sword, Emo's Austin, TX September 17, 2005
Review by Dara

Local band whose description moved me enough to e-mail them for news of next show, very apt musicians who were Black Sabbath so verbatim that you couldn't respect them, but like RecordStoreGirl said with cool non-enthusiasm "They're fun."

From: Dara Shifrer
To: amarx
Subject: RE: I Was There When It Rang
Date: Mon, 12 Sep 2005

I was going to yell at you for being a huge fat e-mail loser, but then I didn't respond to you for what two weeks. EXCEPT - I was moving. What's your excuse Marx?

The move is a hugely positive thing. My old place had been infested with rats for months - the switch in power was finalized while I was in Europe. Ate through 14 boxes of food items, spread their trash and nastiness throughout the kitchen and completely destroyed the back wall of a cupboard. Really horrible.

So now I live in a place with a real floorplan in a very nice neighborhood of Austin. And I am happy every day. Hmph. I'm grumpy today. But, I looked for a long time and finally found a duplex place which I so prefer. The landlady was very hesitant about allowing my cat, but not for the sake of the carpeting and such. She was concerned that he would disrupt the cat order already in place with the cats upstairs. And that's who my landlady is. I called on a leaky faucet a few days ago and she told me that the old tenant never called on it. She didn't notice it when she walked through. I said well... THEN she said, "Have you turned the faucet off all the way?" Bitchy woman.

School is literally relaxed this year. Miniscule classes. Incredible schedule. I'm teaching to low scorers again so behavior will be an issue but when has it not been.

I am very happy for you to hear that you live alone now. So how goes life in Somerville? Job? Social life? I have been curious about you for a long time. I only hear glimpses from Julianna and...

Dara

From: Andrew Marx
To: dshifrer
Subject: RE: I Was There When It Rang
Date: Fri, 16 Sep 2005

I've lived alone in Somerville for about a month now, well, six weeks. Except for the fact that it's hot and muggy, which it would be anyway, and I don't have a television, things are co-pasetic. The bed is soft. I broke it in with the most gorgeous boy I have ever seen naked and he was a lot of fun to boot. It was a weird night. Great conversation, rockin body.

I have a date tonight too, but it's a different guy. This one is tall and a little bigger, but we have a lot in common. Our conversations so far have been about comic books and Tori Amos. You see my point.

It's the weekend, time for me to blow away.

AM

From: Dara Shifrer
To: amarx
Subject: RE: I Was There When It Rang
Date: Tue, 27 Sep 2005

My budget is destroyed by my apartment. I am in severe straits and can't seem to stop myself from the spending. Got paid on the 23rd and am already in the negative by hundreds for the rest of the month. No food this month! I convinced myself that not living in a dumpily decorated apartment had become a priority at this stage in my life. So a better couch. A tablecloth. Shoe organizers. I don't know - it adds up. I'm still a cheap skate. Just skating a little faster.

What kind of guy has a fabulous body and can conversate great? I think you're lying Andy Marx. Don't even talk to me about hot and humid. 108 on Sunday!! It hurt to be outside. It must be some throwback from the hurricane. Oh the drama we have had down here with that. And we're just peripheral. They evacuated Houston in good post-Katrina intention and we got a good number of them. So they were closing schools to use as shelters. Teachers and students at my school were disappointed at not being chosen to shelter. Lots of drama footage of the storm. Newscasters with dripping bodies and hair plastered in a full-head mohawk.

I continue to date the archaeologist Michael. We are not as seamless as when he lived in Belize. I am suddenly a needy insecure complainer. I am disgusted with myself and have stopped that. My mother is aglow with marriage hopings but I e-mailed her today that our chances at that remain at 10%.

Becca called me. I left her a message.

I must eat. Right now.

Dara

From: Andrew Marx
To: dshifrer
Subject: Something Ain't Right
Date: Wed, 28 Sep 2005

Well the boy front hasn't been that successful, but I can't consider them failures either. The one I like cancelled the date, and although he keeps coming back and saying "let's meet again" he works late, isn't feeling well, whatever. He keeps coming up with excuses and then making a point to convey them to me as if that was supposed to express interest (possibly to allay my own insecurities, or more likely, just his own) without commitment. Unfortunately, I really gelled with him the best (or had thought so) so I tried to convey that to him and I'm not sure he quite believed me.

The other, as I referred to him, comic book/Tori Amos lover, we've seen each other a couple times. He's a nice guy but he talks so much, and doesn't seem to retain anything. So we'll basically have the same conversations over and over again and he won't stop talking. He asks questions in a rapid fire pattern and it makes me tired, especially the few that I've already answered. We get along, ostensibly have a lot in common; but I just want him to shut the fuck up. Plus he does things that are admittedly totally illogical, like paying for a gym membership he doesn't use, and buying DVD collections that he won't watch. Then says he never has any money. Well, hello. That's easy to remedy.

Unfortunately, the way I feel is that I don't really have a ton of friends in Somerville and I don't have a ton of boy options so I'm trying to give both of them a few chances. Neither is on a career path (they are both in the 27-28 age range) which is also another strange thing to me because while I'm not objective about the success of my career path, I certainly am on one and I make good money.

Money is tighter because of the living by myself apartment situation (as you yourself are feeling the crush). I went out on a limb and spent my savings on a nice bed, couch set and some minor other furniture and now I am officially done. It was pricey, but I'm comfortable enough and I'll just have to be cautious until I rebuild my savings a little. (A little each paycheck). I don't have any exorbitant travel plans coming up, although I'm going to Delaware for the weekend which will cost some in gas. And then I'll be in California to spend a long weekend with my mother and brother and wife. Also not really a high cost affair except maybe the plane ticket but I bought that a while ago.

I'm trying to keep somewhat busy during my evenings because I don't want to flounder, since I essentially moved to a new city and am still learning my way around. Like someone asks me for a recommendation on food and I know, like, one restaurant nearby.

It's fun being on the dating track, and I think the first date kind of propagates others. I'm also in a class for gay writers and it's interesting and engaging. The teacher is something else. Really articulate and thoughtful one minute, and the next looks like he popped into another universe. He has the gay affectation of seeming to be interested in you but you get the impression he's thinking about the dishes in the sink at home. I found the experience worthwhile though, and the class is all semester once a week, even the homework kind of intrigued me. We have to edit and improve on a piece we wrote quickly during the class describing someone's bedroom.

Mixed bag,

AM

From Concert-Central.com
Stickpony, Carousel Lounge, Austin, TX September 28, 2005
Review by Dara

TheNewHippie's band - their best show ever - escaped me because Rockboy responded to my Christmas invite with news that he and BestGirlFriend had New Year's plans

From: Dara Shifrer
To: amarx
Subject: RE: Something Ain't Right
Date: Thu, 6 Oct 2005

The one that you liked who expresses interest by not going out with you - have you pursued him? Maybe he's playing hard to get. Needs to be convinced that you like him the bestest. Though, what with the e-mail time delay, you might have moved onnnnn. It does seem to be a peculiar coincidence that the dull-side-of-the-fence ones are so available. Rapid-fire-questioning reminded me of myself. Hmph.

I'm pretty friendless myself. I feel like I ought to be trying because Michael leaves the country again soon but eh.

I didn't eat enough fat today and feel eh. And the allergies in Austin this week are monstrous. Felling the oxiest of people. Allergies are so Austin's weak point.

I am on my way to see Corpse Bride, which also pisses me off (lord I am pissy tonight) because I have the money issue. But I guess I have to pay if I want to hang out with Michael.

Tomorrow night is my first opera! Ohh. I am kind of excited. I get to dress up too. I don't know that it will be in English though. Of course it won't. I might just hate it. Greek food before that.

Do you think I ought to go camping this Saturday or keep my penniless self under lock and key?

From: Andrew Marx
To: dshifrer
Subject: RE: Something Ain't Right
Date: Sun, 9 Oct 2005

I'm in California this weekend; staying at my mother's. My brother, the married one, has a lead role in a play we are seeing tonight. Then we have a fancy dinner altogether.

Boys:

> The one that you liked who expresses interest by not going out with you - have you pursued him?

We went out on a second date late Wednesday evening. He wanted to stay in, so we watched America's Next Top Model and then a dreadful movie about this woman that steals $100,000 from her husband and he hires a private eye to get her back. So she convinces her new lover to kill him (which he eventually refuses to do, so she does it and frames the lover). It was a nice night. He didn't seem particularly forthcoming in conversation. But when I said "We should do this again," he hugged me and mumbled something into my shoulder blade. I said, "Was that a yes or no?" And he said when he mumbled it was always a yes.

I don't know if he's shy. I'm not sure. I really enjoy being around him so I guess it doesn't matter. I also can't explain why. We probably have nothing in common. He feels right where other guys usually don't.

His name is Michael, too!

The other one, the talker, has been nixed. My rationale on the one hand is that three dates isn't necessarily enough time to get to know him. On the other hand, I haven't particularly been thrilled with what I have already learned. We disagree so fundamentally about some things; money in particular, that it seems it could be a serious strain to attempting a serious dating relationship (does that sound familiar?)

But in the meantime, a guy at work suddenly expressed interest. Our first date was lunch. We get along really well. He's not really my type physically but that usually doesn't factor in. Meaning I wouldn't pick him out of the crowd if I didn't already know him. The thing is, he shows interest and doesn't make me do all the work. That's big. He planned for us to have an afternoon rendezvous in the park on Thursday (it's a campus holiday).

I don't necessarily need another guy to date but a new friend would be fab. So whether it turns out to be romantic or just platonic, I'm pretty stoked. We are planning a trip to see the leaves in Vermont. I finally found someone to go with me.

From: Dara Shifrer
To: amarx
Subject: RE: Something Ain't Right
Date: Sat, 15 Oct 2005

I didn't realize your brother was an actor. I saw my first opera last weekend and what a wailing disappointment it was. Lame plot (lyrics in English). The mingling of orchestra with voice was interesting for a while until it was same mingling forever and ever. I also had a coughing fit and was not allowed to return until intermission after stepping into the lobby. Whatever. Like a slice of light was going to stop the art in motion. I read a bad review so it may be that one poor choice was the lifetime ruin of opera for me.

"And he said when he mumbled it was always a yes." What a darling! I hope you've seen him since.

Work remains very bizarrely relaxed. I whiled (?...you know what I mean).. the day away in my five-year-plan for attempting to apply to grad school. I am such a lame girl when it comes to making life decisions. It's such a momentous chore for me though. Like an occupation for the elite only or those willing to sacrifice their lives to pursue the degree and I'm not sure I'm that on-fire for the academic life.

Michael and I went to the monthly wine-tasting party last night. It's a good time. People are on a strict drinking schedule and are swiftly moved into much more entertaining realms than they might otherwise occupy. I am the official note-taker which I enjoy.

We had our weekly fight on Thursday. In essence, I told him that I was upset that he doesn't have enough time for me and he told me that he doesn't want to see me sometimes because I'm always upset with him. How circuitous is that...he's such a good debater. Or at least a determined debater. He will not be told that I too believe my behavior dabbles in the ugly female pools.

Tonight there is a Full Moon Party. I hope you're smirking. I have mostly been in the mood to sit in my new apartment with my sore-crusty cat and read my growing stack of magazines.

From Concert-Central.com
The Adicts, Emo's, Austin, TX October 15, 2005
Review by Dara

Rockboy was so excited to see this shticky punk band, they dress Clockwork Orange style with the lead in white face paint but unfortunately their depth ends there, I am apparently not a fan of "anthemic" "oi! Punk" - how is it punk to sing en masse to lame lyrics? - I hate solidarity of any kind...in brief

From: Andrew Marx
To: dshifrer
Subject: RE: Something Ain't Right
Date: Fri, 4 Nov 2005

You ever been to NYC? Come up some time. We'll party like it's 1999.

I've gone through more dating boys than I have rolls of paper towel in my house. I bought a Costco size of paper towels months ago and I think I've gone through two rolls, maybe a third somewhere...The boy disappeared. I think he had health issues or something, but no return calls, no e-mails. I then got involved with someone at work, that was kind of a disaster. Very needy, a little immature and definitely a bad listener. A group of us (him included) are hanging out tonight. A few days ago, I basically had to break up with him (not that I thought we were "going out" but he did somehow) and we'll see how it goes.

From Concert-Central.com
Tia Carrera, Room 710, Austin, TX November 4, 2005
Review by Dara

Just glorious, Rockboy played Pink Floyd's Metal for me to prove the influence, the only band I want to see again and again and again.

From: Dara Shifrer
To: amarx
Subject: RE: Something Ain't Right
Date: Sat, 12 Nov 2005

I have only been to New York for a total of eight hours and am very enticed by your offer to party like it's 1999. I didn't realize that you are that familiar with New York. I do want to go there again - the intensity is palpable, right?

I am trying to decide what to do with my life when I quit teaching and it's depressing me to start this same old scene over again. I would guess that you understand. Michael is incredibly driven in an unpleasantly single-lane focused way, but I don't feel the want to be in the side-basket. Or whatever they call those little motorcycle side seats.

I am curious as to how the meeting with the fresh ex- went. Do you date within the same circle a lot? Most people do and it gives rise to a lot of interesting social situations.

I am supposedly on my way to see a country rock band in a bar with scary circus elephants painted on the walls.

Bye!

Dara

From: Andrew Marx
To: dshifrer
Subject: RE: Something Ain't Right
Date: Mon, 21 Nov 2005

NYC (well Manhattan) is scary, but it's kind of like a scary movie, or an amusement park ride. For the most part, it's scary fun. It's controlled-environment scares. It's so huge and so many people and everyone running in every direction. You think chaos, but there's a scheme behind it. I always said that I really would probably like NYC a lot more if I saw it from the perspective of a native. The only native I know is my step-mother, who doesn't exactly scream 'fun' to me. But my brother is moving there for grad school and then maybe some day he will be like a native.

But I can get there in four hours and that means even spending a day or an overnight there no problem. Any time you like. My next scheduled visit is in the middle of March for a wedding. I'll definitely be in Somerville through August of next year, but then I have to make some major life decisions. I like my apartment well enough, although I need to figure out the air conditioning fiasco for next summer. So how long have you been officially dating Michael? Do you call him Mike at all? You make him sound stuffy so I don't suppose he does nicknames.

The fresh-ex and I are feeling our way through friendship rituals. The problem I had all along is he advanced our so-called relationship to levels of intensity that I wasn't sharing, and after a couple of weeks. That's not a couple weeks of dating. That's, I met you two weeks ago. Plus, he wasn't a very good listener. And I totally was not attracted to him. It was a little awkward, but he had convinced himself it was so intense that when it comes down to it, it makes sense that it would be awkward. I have no idea what he thinks about the 'just be friends' notion but I can't worry about it. I really want to date a couple of his close friends, but one thing at a time. And no, I don't usually date within the same circles. Usually, I never hear from the guy again. In this case, I am highly amused to try it.

We have ravens outside our window on the second floor. Loads of them. I guess they don't migrate. Work is busy, like insane busy but of course, I'm showing up for work late and sending e-mails. Tonight, I may have been invited to a Monday Night Football watching party. That's like heaven for me.

AM

From: Dara Shifrer
To: amarx
Subject: RE: Something Ain't Right
Date: Thu, 1 Dec 2005

How many weddings can one gay man go to?

You seem to be a constant buzz of travel and events but maybe that is Dara's version of Andy's life.

And what, exactly, is the AC fiasco? If it is truly a fiasco, and you are renting, shouldn't the landlords be paying for new units? Or have you BOUGHT a condo?

Andy Marx does not want just ONE of the friends of the ex, he wants a COUPLE of them. I thought that was so funny. How has that worked out?

Michael and I have dated since January. I do believe that we have broken up though as of Monday or last Friday. He will be putting work ahead of me.

Luckily, my time and mind are relieved and consumed with applications to grad school. It's another fruitless gesture at meaning in my life, eh? The applying is good jolly fun though. I don't remember when my evenings have been so full.

Tell me more, tell me more,

Dara

From: Andrew Marx
To: dshifrer
Subject: Call if You Want Something
Date: Mon, 5 Dec 2005

My new band of the day is Our Lady Peace.

> How many weddings can one gay man go to?

I'm done until March.

> You seem to be a constant buzz of travel and events but maybe that is Dara's version of Andy's life.

I am going to England to visit my sister for a week around Christmas. I have two weeks off around that time, and if I sat at home in Somerville for the whole thing, I might slit my wrists. I'll probably sit around my sister's small burg for a week, but at least it's a change of scenery. I think she's taking most of the days off.

> And what, exactly, is the AC fiasco?

It's hot in my apartment and I don't have air conditioning.

> If it is truly a fiasco, and you are renting, shouldn't the landlords be paying for new units?

Doesn't work that way. Air conditioning units are the responsibility of the tenant. But I moved in August, so I suffered through it for the duration of the summer, which this year was interminable.

> Or have you BOUGHT a condo?

No.

> Andy Marx does not want just ONE of the friends of the ex, he wants a COUPLE of them. I thought that was so funny. How has that worked out?

I flirted with one of the younger ones (probably 25 years old) and hung out with them en masse. It's a long term project; everyone sort of disperses during the winter. Meanwhile, the ex- isn't showing much interest in hanging out with me, as is his wont.

We do occasionally chat or catch up on e-mail though. I think he feels guilty if he ignores me.

> Michael and I have dated since January. I do believe that we have broken up though as of Monday or last Friday. He will be putting work ahead of me.

I do hate ambiguity. Whatever happened, I hope it was what you were looking for. I think good relationships don't take work, at least not in the sense that it feels right. It should feel good, you know, without a lot of soul-searching? That can come later. I shared this theory with my ex- and he wasn't impressed. He's a selective listener.

AM

From: Dara Shifrer
To: amarx
Subject: RE: Call if You Want Something
Date: Mon, 12 Dec 2005

Becca's so smart Andy. I didn't recognize it in her before. I knew I liked talking to her but she's razor sharp. Not perceptive always, in regards to herself, but aren't we all not...Anyway

> Meanwhile, the ex- isn't showing much interest in hanging out with me, as is his wont.

Ex s that really loved you will never show interest in hanging out. They are defeated and shamed and mourning...

> I think good relationships don't take work, at least not in the sense that it feels right. It should feel good, you know, without a lot of soul-searching? That can come later. I shared this theory with my ex- and he wasn't impressed.

But that is exactly the problem and the non-problem! Being with Michael took no work in the beginning - we understood each other perfectly within our first three hours. He loves Twin Peaks, music, culture, argument,... It was so seamless and flawless, it frightened me. But we turned into a logistical nightmare. Working out time and futures... I hate all pat answers right now, so I, also, am not impressed. ;-)

I had a day of fierce nostalgia for you for some reason last week. Realized what a good part of my life you are. Ah Andy!

With fond and warm regards,

Dara

From: Andrew Marx
To: dshifrer
Subject: RE: Call if You Want Something
Date: Wed, 14 Dec 2005

Random mention of Becca. Have you talked?

Whatever Becca says about me, she is stuck in this perception of Andy circa 1999. It's like a painting that she's always staring at, trying to find new meaning out of an old image. I tend to recycle my themes, but she tends to recycle the fact that I recycle my themes. If you get my meaning. I think we are stuck with who we are, however that may be. She gets, stubborn is the word, stuck. She gets stuck a lot. And her breaking point is so high, she is indomitable. I am always amazed at her inner strength.

I think that we grow and mature, but we always come back to the things that haunt us the most. I have no idea how you beat those demons. In fact, I have accepted my demons and I now bathe in them. (Maybe that's a little counterproductive, and that does occur to me on occasion - but there you go, I'm more mellow because of it). Now, there is a vision of my 30's. I'll be fruitful when I get around to it, damnit.

Ah, but don't all these random musings sound familiar?

Was Michael good-looking?

AM

From: Dara Shifrer
To: amarx
Subject: I'll be fruitful when I get around to it, damnit.
Date: Tue, 3 Jan 2006

Speaking of Becca and you (well, speaking near 17 days ago), she did mention a date of yours for the first time that I'd ever heard. It has always annoyed me that she seemed ignorant of your love/ sex life. Ignorant by choice I thought.

I'm exhausted today but have been for a week it seems. Michael and I are apparently together again (I do feel bad for the former info but it did seem permanent) and he keeps horrible hours that I can't handle. He is senselessly more sexy to me than anyone that I have dated. Your question made me laugh. Where did it come from?

My cat is suffering some sort of existential crisis. A decrease in self-respect it appears to me. He has been tufting his white hair all over the house when I am gone and then when let outside, immediately wallows in the dirt. He may be angry with me for my poor ownership skills. Or the neighboring cat insulted him.

I returned from the besmogged and trafficked Southern California last Wednesday. It charms less and less. I enjoy the smeltering diversity of people but my area is horrifying. Addled with drugs and ignorance. Even my family I think. Not as much as the rest of Them but certainly increasingly influenced. Maybe it is just advancing age. My uncle who came out two years ago visited as well as the new conservative hick boyfriend of my sister. And the whole hick family. Politics were not discussed - nor were religion, sexuality, taste in cuisine... I sound snobby but I didn't feel that I belonged. My sister's boyfriend's family did not even know that she had a second sister. Not that I would ever return. It was actually a very good visit. My family is doing well - seem to be on a stable swell.

I stayed up late on New Year's Eve but not doing anything fantastic. Saw a one-man band and ate crappy buffet food at a local bar. The downtown scene was not to be tolerated. OH! Try and catch the Rollergirls special on A&E. It's a whole series on the roller derby scene in Austin. It's particularly enjoyable for me because I have been to the games and see the girls about town and it's my town, but I think it would make you laugh too.

Otherwise, I spend my spare time applying for graduate school. With much enjoyment. Teaching resumes tomorrow. I am bereft. Egh. Hopefully just one more semester.

What goes on in your life?

Pick up

Andy,

Who are you now? ;-) Your website is so professional and different from previous sites. I wonder what inspired all of this -

What I mean to say, is, Congratulations! It's great! I look forward to seeing where it all leads.

I am absolutely submerged in school work. I miss having private time but am still interested enough in the work that I do not regret the leaving of teaching. I keep saying that to remind myself. Sorry if I've told you that repeatedly.

Send me some Andy news too!

:-) Dara

From: Andrew Marx
To: dshifrer
Subject: RE: Long Shot
Date: Thu, 19 Oct 2006

When you asked about inspiration - I am facing my 30's and found my life to be insipid. It's pretty much that. I needed a forum for my writing, and I wanted it to be professional-looking, instead of just another LiveJournal.

Unfortunately, for other news, there is scant.

From Concert-Central.com
Jenny Lewis and the Watson Twins, Stubb's, Austin, TX October 24, 2006
Review by Dara

The easiest loveliest voice in creation. Peoples' chord music from country to croons to lite girl rock. Wise lyrics that made me tear. I just love a good female performer. Purports to be from Las Vegas but web stuff says LA but seems to be from the South. Very tiny and there was something of the annoying precious superstar to her. Watson Twins not worth their weight - couldn't keep a beat and one of their voices broke on one of two solos.

4

Chapter Four *Pick Up The Receiver,*
I'll Make You A Believer

---- Original Message ----
From: Andrew Marx
To: dshifrer
Subject: Dare to dream
Date: Tue, 24 Jan 2006

Okay, so here's my dream. *First, I have to go to a going away party for a coworker. He wants me to sit close to the front (of the stage?) to admire his coin collection. I think I have his speech in my hands, but it's definitely a couple sheets of paper. I go to the temple for the ceremony but kids are there in Hebrew school, in every room so I walk in and out among them. Then I see the going away party has been moved outside near a pond. On the way, I run into my father and his wife, his daughter and my sister. My sister is wearing a very pretty dress and I ask her what she is doing there, and she says that she wants me to come with her to Vermont if I have the time. Then his daughter says we better hurry because as soon as my step-sister is done performing, the going away party starts. I got the impression that my "co-worker" was a wealthy Jew, as though explaining why we were there.*

I woke up and watched about an hour of World Poker Championship then went back to bed.

So I dream that I am among a new group of friends, who are a little secret society. So they finally take me to their hideout, which is where they raise little toddlers. Everyone is a little tense. I walk around the property, and am told by this big black lady to keep off of the children's play things. I see an oversized toilet out of which rises a man (a bounty hunter, I deduce) and I sense danger and go looking for my friends who have gone outside but are not there when I get there. The kids and the adults are all in a panic and finally I see my friends at the top of a hill (think like an outpost) in a structure that is against the wood fence (very high) surrounding the property. I make my way up as the hunter starts throwing bombs of gelatin that melt then explode. I yell at my new friends for deserting me and disappearing into their secret clubhouse while all this is going on. One of them asks me if I was told how to defeat the bounty hunter, the black lady screams and the dream ends as we try to escape over the fence.

So there you go.

So New Year's. I spent time with my sister. Her town is cute. It is a very small town on the ocean, and all the "convenience stores" are what passes for shopping trips. I think my sister and husband grocery at the convenience store next door but it's small and quaint and I couldn't tell if it sells anything that, say, Shaw's or Ralph's sells. Except milk. It definitely sells milk. But their version of "Wal Mart" is five little corner stores that mostly duplicate the same aisle of candy, toys and dvds (of which a remarkably diverse collection is for sale in these tiny stores). The first night was a bank holiday so nothing was open, but we found a pub and went for Indian.

It snowed! They declared a state of emergency after the first half inch (think the top tenth of your fingernail and that's about what sticks on the ground) which I laughed at of course, but they get snow rarely so it's a serious event!

Then Megan and I stayed in London for two days. We did Harrods and every Gap in the West End and Piccadilly and Portabello Road, which was a total disappointment. It was cold and the stands were just selling crap and it looked more like East LA than Santa Monica.

My job experience has slowly and inexorably sunk to new lows which is disappointing. I'm harboring a lot of anger issues these days.

Ha!

AM

From: Dara Shifrer
To: amarx
Subject: RE: Dare to dream
Date: Mon, 06 Feb 2006

What a fantastic e-mail. I've been waiting for some great dream to respond with but...eh...my dreams are all fluff from my days. Minutiae. Social drama. I'm a stress ball and superficial as all hell possibly. Your dream was fantastic really. What did it mean? I would guess that you didn't try to explore it at all. Have you ever seen the HBO series Carnivàle? It could be an episode. No, too twisted. Your dream I mean. I would like to see you. Visit I mean. I ran across a photo of you in an old old album and you looked so different (very young), much more Marxish. You looked a lot like your brothers, probably because they're the age you were then. We are terribly old now. There's a really slim chance I might be coming up to the Boston area this summer. But if I do, please be prepared to spend time with an old friend.

BUT, last night...it was a very sweet evening. Breezy but warm and I had opened all of my windows. A cold front swept in later, but it was a Texas cold front mind you and only served to heighten my good sleep and dreams. And I dreamt that I heard a piano note sounding again and again. Not quickly but in slow measure. I didn't remember the dream until I heard the notes again once woken. There was still a low breeze that only intensified the eeriness. It was absolutely not a chime. Just a steady regular full...piano note. When I heard rustling near my window, I fancied a gnome or goblin by my window carrying a portable organ or keyboard. I was in sufficiently whimsy enough a mood to open the door very quickly to let my Crahobi out so as not to let anything in. I still haven't solved the mystery.

My eyes are twitching during the day which denotes too little sleep or too much stress. I am definitely sleeping enough so am stressing too much. Not sure over what. I am working lots of various little jobs and am in high-maintenance mode, but may just be negotiating relations with Michael long-term. I am ready to be in grad school. I do hope that it happens. My life quality does hang in the balance. How is your job?

My old Austin friend - Oh! who was married to the likely-gay very literate guy whose e-mail I sent to you once b/c he was such a good writer and I thought you would appreciate it - is also a good writer herself and she participates in a creative blog. She has tried to enlist me and I participated a bit but haven't felt moved since. You ought to. You may hate the idea, since you have a fabulous website of your own, but here's the link:

Egh never mind - I can't find link - will send it later!

Hope you're well,

Dara

From: Andrew Marx
To: dshifrer
Subject: RE: Dare to dream
Date: Tue, 07 Feb 2006

Not well, continued job stress. I'm being sent into workplace exile shortly. Oh but nevermind. You don't want to hear about that. Does everyone have a dream like this? Mine takes place in this haunted house with many bats and dark corners and creatures of the deep and there is always an old teacher of mine lurking about like a phantom. I visited that house every single year just before the start of school. The details varied very little, just the face of the teacher - though it was always one of my instructors. I miss that damn house.

I'm intrigued by the gnome carrying a portable organ. Perhaps you should have let him in and let him lull you into a peaceful sleep. Not so much if it was a goblin, up to mischief those are.

You tease me with visits to Boston but I know it's just that. Don't worry, I don't hold it against you. I remain humbly caught up in the day to day of...well, the day to day stuff, I guess. You know that I post to a blog through my MySpace account? It's amusing to write freeform, no rhyme or reason to my musings, very much in the LiveJournal vein. People read it though and then I think, maybe I should have done some selective editing.

I know you don't have a myspace account, maybe I'll send you a sample. Maybe it will provide some cheer...

Andrew

From Where's Andrew? Blog, MySpace.com
Thursday, February 16, 2006
4:18 AM - Hammer Down
Current mood: bouncy

I woke this morning and somehow between getting out of bed with my alarm and getting out of the shower and drying off my crotch, I got it into my head that I was running late. So I figured I wouldn't make the 8:30 train (my regular) and settle for the nine o five train instead. I rush rush rush, blow my nose, organize my briefcase, discover my phone in the pocket of my jacket, check the temperature outside, make a sandwich, head out the door and stop short. I still had another forty extra minutes this morning to make the 8:30 train!

I just wrote a song called "A Little Coffee on My Crotch (Have a Nice Day)." It's a little bit M People and a little bit Kaiser Chiefs. The chorus goes "I just spilled coffee on my crotch. Have a nice day! Have a nice day! I just built a city from the rot. Have a nice day! Have a nice day!"

I think it will be a b-side to my hit single "I'm Not Listening Anyway" which I think will be in stores in March ahead of the full album cleverly titled "You're Not Listening Anyway." We are filming the video this weekend between the outbound and inbound tracks on the Fitchburg line at Park and Beacon in Somerville, MA. It's mostly just me spinning around in circles mumbling lyrics I don't remember intercut with a group of my friends watching the half time show concert footage of the Rolling Stones at the Super Bowl right around the time Mick Jagger's shirt doesn't quite cover his stomach. I'm still waiting for the rights to use the footage but I'm fairly confident I will get to use it because nobody would remember the Super Bowl performance for anything else otherwise. It was about as exciting as watching the same thirty seconds of When a Stranger Calls during every commercial break for the last three weeks. "Did you check on the children?!?" No fucker, go check on them yourself. Spoiler alert, the murderer is not the father.

Not to mention the sound mix at the half time show was wretched. You'd get better sound off an 8-track.

The video for "I'm Not Listening Anyway" is being directed by the homeless guy that sleeps every night at the bus stop (line 83) at Porter Square, on the east side facing the Blockbuster Video. I asked him if he knows how to use a camcorder and he gave me a very dense stare. I think maybe he thought I was eyeballing his grocery basket of discarded amarays. (Google the word, I ain't no dictionary.) All he has to do is press the button on the camcorder and not run off with it and we're golden. I can do the editing later. I am paying him in packages of Goldfish crackers because they are on sale for $1.50 each at the Star Market this week.

Insert Smiley!

Currently watching :
Tori Amos - Video Collection: Fade to Red
Release date: 14 February, 2006

0 Comments - 0 Kudos - Add Comment - Edit - Remove

From: Dara Shifrer
To: amarx
Subject: RE: Dare to dream
Date: Sun, 19 Feb 2006

Andy, where does the time go? My most recent time was spent on a Letter to the Editor of The Atlantic Monthly over an article on the increase in random blow jobs amongst young girls. That was not the thing, though - the thing was that the female author used words like "whore" and "streetwalker" and "messy blowjobs" (exposing herself as a sexual inhibit). It was great fun to write, despite the likelihood that they'll ignore it just as they ignored my first letter to the editor. A great magazine in its dull plodding way.

My infrequent e-mails to you are more explicative than most of the long-term relationships that I maintain. I am considering the road trip options for me this summer and finances are the biggest determinant - it's not looking good, but rest assured that you will be notified. In sum, we may not know when we will meet, but, meet again, we always will. I realize our enduring kindredness more and more as we grow OLD.

Becca. I called her on a whim on a lonely Valentine's Day with a stupid message and she delighted me with a callback. She repeats her life incessantly. She is smart and insightful, except for when it comes to herself. But isn't that the story of everybody. But Becca, I always feel, is this untapped vessel of depth and warmth. She just needs the exactly right kind of manipulation.

Oh, Please send me a mix CD. Nobody does it anymore. Especially the Blue October breakdown song. Genuine music - I love it. Do you want a mix from me? Oh! I shouldn't promise b/c my computer is a piece of everliving crap that cannot consistently burn to save its everliving life. Someday Andy someday.

How's the job that sounds so horrible?

With respect and affection,

Dara

From: Andrew Marx
To: dshifrer
Subject: RE: Dare to dream
Date: Tue, 21 Feb 2006

I'll make you a disc. Give me a week or so (mostly to get it to a mailbox - the discs could be done today). Try to find some unique and odd-ducks in my collection. Of course, I always think it's off the wall and then it's really not. But. That Blue October song has gone from moving me to tears to filling me with joy when I hear it. So it goes.

I'm trying to juggle a ton of things right now (like, this very minute) least of all is a presentation that I have at 2pm that is about half-formed. I know exactly what I need to do to prepare, which is why I'm not overly concerned. I am better at making the list than doing it though.

Work was fine last week, weirdly positive vibes. That's the thematic gist of work right now. I generally work best when I know what the outcome is that I want and I finally reached that point over the weekend, a lot thanks to Becca who started spouting Andy-isms at me that I used to live by. *Don't worry about things you have no control over, and if you don't plan on doing anything about a problem, then don't whine about it.* Duly noted and applied. I am a better man. Who would have thought such wisdom from her? She's right of course, particularly as how it applies to me (another one: most problems are transitory, and in this case, mine certainly 100% are).

By the by, I never meant to imply that our relationship is not special. I happen to like you a lot as a person, and I have to tell you, there aren't that many people in my universe that I would say that sincerely to. Even members of my own family don't qualify.

Well, it's now about thirty minutes later than I wanted to start working on this presentation so I best get the get-out and go. AM

From Where's Andrew? Blog, MySpace.com
Saturday, February 25, 2006
10:14 AM - Ten
Current mood: enthralled
Category: Travel and Places

1. Why is it on a fifty-minute flight, people can't manage to stay in their seats for the whole flight? I mean, for the twelve minutes that the captain turned off the fasten seat belt sign, it was a line to the bathroom that made the wait for Episode III tickets look brief.

2. They really need to fix the lines at Logan's Terminal C check-in area. In between a line (crowd) of people waiting to speak with an actual human, and a line of people with a boarding pass and luggage, queuing to pass their luggage in, was a thick cluster of us trying to get a boarding pass at the self-help kiosks, of twelve, only three were actually working! But absolutely no rhyme or reason (or stanchions for that matter) to keep the three lines from intermingling. And while I would love to blame this

on the airlines, I really think at least 50% of the blame is the layout of Terminal C.

3. Calling your in-flight attendants 'world class' does not mean they actually are world class, that any customer will believe they are world class, no matter how many times you say it. (And I don't subscribe to the theory that 'world class' is actually referring to the fact that the airline flies to other countries once in a while.)

4. Speaking of. 'in-flight attendants' versus 'flight attendants'. I sincerely hope they are actually in the plane, and not hanging out in the baggage compartment.

5. The in-flight attendant chided me for not putting my seat up before take-off, even after I told her, and then DEMONSTRATED to her that the seat was broken and even the slightest amount of pressure flipped me backwards. Then she spent the rest of the flight (admittedly barely another hour of our otherwise mutually exclusive lives together) glaring at me every time she walked by. When I asked for a cookie, she tossed it at me as if I had rabies.

I won't say which airline...

6. JFK is a perfect microcosm of NYC itself. I think it should be on a list of must-see tourist attractions.

7. In this order: Snow fall, de-ice the plane, take off. Then, the woman behind me asks her son "Is it raining outside?"

8. The captain's apology because JFK ordered us to circle in the air for ten minutes? "It's not my fault they switched runways on us." I need a t-shirt with that on it.

9. The gate agent could not match my reservation with my frequent flyer account because one was under my nickname. His solution? Change my name on the reservation (which fortunately, I suppose, I was already at the gate so from a security perspective, acceptable, but I can't help but think that there is something a little dubious about just arbitrarily changing someone's name on the itinerary.)

10. The mother behind me also seemed confused about why she couldn't get to watch movies on our fifty minute flight. The inflight attendant had to explain to her, HAD TO EXPLAIN TO HER that the flight wasn't long enough to see the whole movie.

Currently reading :
Everything Is Illuminated
By Jonathan Safran Foer
Release date: 31 May, 2003

0 Comments - 0 Kudos - Add Comment - Edit - Remove

From: Dara Shifrer
To: amarx
Subject: Bumpersticker - "SUVs promote terrorism" - flush on the fat backside of an SUV
Date: Sun, 26 Feb 2006

MySpace is a terror. Formalized social stratification and personal interactions on a public forum. It makes me nauseous in a way that makes me proud of myself. Not too many convictions left - always happy to see one pop up.

Yeah for the mix! This Blue October song is just full of wonderfulness apparently. I cannot wait. My burner has crapped out, once again. It enrages me, so I can't stay on this topic for very long. I need a new computer, is the fact, and think it will be a laptop. What kind would you suggest? I do basic word processing, e-mail, internet, and lots of music doo-dadding.

I have two pieces of news that are exciting and life-transforming enough that they are waking me up at night, in terror. I got into grad school. UT Austin. Sociology department. I am terribly excited for all of that, except that the "great" offer that they made is not seeming that way to me. I will have to live at half my already measly salary as a teacher, get a part-time job on top of a 20-hour TA job, or take out some $15K/year in loans. I'm not sure if I'm being unreasonable as to how all of this works - actually I'm fairly certain that I am being unreasonable. To my shame, the other downfall in my wayward female head, is that this commitment may exact great costs on current and future relationships.

With that segueway, Michael found me a job at this worksite (Maya ruin digging) for the month of June. So I will be working as a Lab Director during his summer session. Besides curtailing our separation, I will get to STUDY ABROAD FINALLY AFTER ALL OF THESE YEARS!!! It will be the closest quarters in which Michael and I have coexisted, so in its twisted way, will also exact a cost on current and future relationships.

I am riding on a little wave of high. No more teaching Andy. I will miss aspects of it because I love aspects, but dear Jesus, bring on the adult interaction and the removal of my 8-hour stage.

So what happened with the job business?

From: Andrew Marx
To: dshifrer
Subject: Original
Date: Thu, 16 Mar 2006

Congrats on grad school. Yay for a new direction and you get to escape the horrible, well-behaved children. I don't think you are supposed to be able to live comfortably during grad school, although you could always get married. Then you have the benefit of a second income to pay your rent and such. I know a few people who have done it that way but I suppose that would fall into your category of also exacting a cost on current and future relationships.

Most of my friends in grad school make shit, teach part time and have loans. It's designed to beat you down and then build you up anew.

You always have the most interesting summers lined up. I skipped that phase of my life. Do you get to take pictures of Mayan ruins? That would be exciting. Maybe you should do a Mayan ruin blog. Or take your guitar and write music channeling the Mayan musical tradition. You could be the next Shakira.

On to more mundane things:

Myspace is entertainment. I don't really use it intending to make friends, but I have found a few guys who have entertained me with e-mails and posts. What I realized reading other people's blogs, some of them are really hardcore into detailing events and other people are hardcore into detailing their emotions about things happening to them. Nobody really falls in-between. I might be doing something wrong...I have no perspective if my writing is entertainment, but I aim to provide a good chuckle.

You probably already went through the buying experience in the time it took me to respond, but: Basic laptops are cheap these days, and light weight. Mine is expensive and heavy, but it is like an industrial laptop. Dell is pretty much universal. I would just go to a computer store you trust and buy what they got. If you go directly to Dell.com or gateway, your warranty will be better and your customer service support as well (I say that since you have trust issues with your computer).

This e-mail wasn't so exciting. Try again next time!

Andy

From: Dara Shifrer
To: amarx
Subject: RE: Original
Date: Sun, 26 Mar 2006

Firstly, I received not one, but two, CDs from you!!! I am still working at getting the listening in but they appear to have the quality that I have come to expect from Andy mixes. Thanks very much. And as soon as I get my computing troubles in line, I have plans for you!

Are your friends happy that they chose grad school? I am so conflicted about it at the moment. A little conflicted about everything at the moment maybe. I went to the orientation and was suffused in excitement for the first half and then just tired and overwhelmed for the second. It seems like a lot of great conversations and ideas but I am not sure how useful it all is. In the end, I am a girl who hopes to be useful. Whatever that means. And the money remains a big concern. I think I got a good offer as far as UT offers go, but after being a working person, going into that kind of debt while living on a strict budget is very unpleasant to me. Maybe it wouldn't be as unpleasant if I was sure that I was doing something that would bring me to better and happier heights. I guess I can't, at this point, see the point in not going on with it.

Are you mocking the Maya Andy? They were a very important people. Astronomy, math, written language and, of course, penis puncturing. I did have a picture of a ruin but I think I lost it. I just downloaded my first set of 85 photos from my first ever digital camera. It was thrilling. Except I remain appalled at what I look like in fine-grain high quality photographs - I definitely don't look high quality.

I hear tales that you went to a fairytale wedding recently. Do tell. I am going to be a bridesmaid for the first time this autumn. I was unreasonably excited (for a person who doesn't believe in weddings and possibly marriage)...until I got the price tag! And my friend says in the e-mail to not let finances be a concern and to please let her know if we'd like her to pay. Yeah, and forever be branded the lout who wouldn't buy the bridesmaid dress. I did spend a couple of hours trying to come up with excuse to get myself out of it.

My life has been extraordinarily busy for the last several weeks. I'm pretty tired of it but created it all too. Tutored for three hours Saturday morning - the same two 8th grade boys! Three hours! It wasn't that bad actually. Kind of Breakfast Club. One was a small gangster with diamond earrings and the other was slightly mad and tangential. And me.

Speaking of side jobs, I typed for my dyslexic love-seeker this morning. He actually e-mailed a 30 year old today (he's 56 and usually refuses to go below 45). Made both of us uncomfortable - striking a little too close to home. Michael tells me he only pretends to loftily restrain himself to contacting only women of a suitable age because he knows damn well that the young ones won't take him.

I didn't tell my mother I was going to Belize - none of her financial business and she doesn't understand why I need to travel. She became distraught when she couldn't reach me and put out an APB on me, EVEN THOUGH my sisters knew and could tell her exactly where I was. Of course, the latter happened first and the former happened in motherly vengeance. So we spoke for the first time today after several tense e-mails and she said she was trying to reach me because she needed to tell me that soy milk contributes to incidents of breast cancer. I said, "Mmm. Thanks." She persisted by reminding me that my aunt died of breast cancer and with that kind of family history... "Yes

yes," I said. She just really thinks that I should immediately cease the consumption of soy milk or tofu. "Yes, of course." Very passive-aggressive. She knew I was yessing her in a blow off of a conversation I would never win and I knew she was persisting to irritate me as much as possible. Mothers.

How's yours?

;-) Dara

From: Andrew Marx
To: dshifrer
Subject: RE: Original
Date: Fri, 31 Mar 2006

So it's sixty degrees outside, and the building has the heat on. I am roasting. I can't leave for another fifteen minutes (well, okay, I can leave and just sit at the train station, but otherwise, there is nothing but to sit there). Then, I thought I had already written a reply to this e-mail, but that doesn't appear to be the case. Plus, the Indian I had for lunch is taking revenge on me in burp formation.

My friends in grad school almost universally adore it for both being a tremendous opportunity and a challenge. It is the dual aspect of being poor and underappreciated that appeals to their liberal souls. They love to discuss the minutiae of student behavior and research activities and their own suffering. I love it, I love being around them.

I can relate to the money woes of the bridesmaid. The whole everything about weddings is

Okay, so now it is Friday (above was all written on Thursday). I am really struggling to respond to your e-mail. I hate weddings. But the last one I went to was actually really heartfelt and emotional for me. I didn't cry or anything, but I was feeling sentimental. And a lot of people I knew or met in college were there. Weddings are a scam, for sure, but it's also a scam on the guests, who are pumped for every possible dime. Scam on the couple who pay through the nose for all the same things that cost less if your event is not a wedding. I think it is all incalculably worse for the bridesmaids, according to my sister who seems to score bridesmaid status pretty regularly (although less so now that she's in another country).

I think you ought to embrace your grad school experience. It definitely is a way different world than just being a workaday individual, in any capacity. It puts you in a different mindset, allows you to dream and explore under a safe umbrella. I just spilled coffee all over my shirt, thank God it is dark blue. I'm dressed down today because I am taking my student workers to the Museum of Science. Am I the best boss or what?

But as far as the wedding thing, I think you should really consider being honest with the bride and work something out. Not, I can't pay for it, but maybe, can you help me out, or split the costs, or pay up front and I will pay you back. Something. It's not worth the stress and I think girls in particular, are really silly about the whole mystique of weddings. Everyone knows it's expensive, and she did offer.

94

My mother, since you asked, is starting a new job next week, is absolutely ecstatic about it. It was pretty bad at her last job (which I think today is her last day) because her boss was a moron.

Myself, I am in a good place right now. In a week, I'm heading to Bennington in Vermont to see a man about a job. Go rural living! I'm a little excited about the possibility but the logistics of breaking my lease and buying a car and physically moving - a little overwhelming. Also, it's really a bit anticipatory because I don't have a job offer yet and so I can only speculate.

That be all. AM

From SmartReMarx.com
Wedding Tales: It All Begins Somewhere March 23, 2006
Posted by Andrew

This wedding tale begins with the groom. I met him in college. His favorite story about me is that my first sentence to him was "Fuck you." He said something that ticked me off, provoked me into that kind of response to a stranger. What was it? It doesn't matter; he was that kind of person. (Still is). Later on, I loaned him a blanket to use.

Flash forward to a few years later.

Okay, the bride entered the picture through a secretive office romance. It is always difficult as a third party to fully realize what attracts two people together. Some couples are mirror images of each other. Identical twins with identical temperaments. Like someone standing next to a mirror and performing all the motions of life with their reflection mimicking every movement.

The other end of the spectrum, and this fits better for Groom and Bride, are polar opposites that are united by some invisible rope. One is the pole and the other is the tether ball. As the ball gets punched around, the other keeps the relationship grounded. Some couples switch their roles back and forth. Some are always the pole, some always the ball.

I like Groom and Bride both. I am acutely aware of their individual idiosyncrasies. He has never been on time to save his life, or anybody else's. I'm being generous. She's a smoker. Yuck. But they are both loyal friends and I love being invited over for dinner because it means I eat better than if I cook for myself.

Is that all you need to know? I will be driving down for the wedding rehearsal, then the wedding is on a Saturday, and coming back home Sunday afternoon. It all sounds simple and linear. Funny how in the planning, most of life does.

Every good wedding story begins somewhere. I don't know how they met, or what they saw in each other; this is my tale after all. So for me the story begins, truly begins, just before the grand event itself.

From SmartReMarx.com
Wedding Tales: Ceremony March 25, 2006
Posted by Andrew

Continental breakfast cracks me up. A danish, a muffin and a banana walk into a bar...So I'm at breakfast and it's Saturday morning. My roommate for the weekend, another groomsman, is still blissfully snoring away and a handful of wedding guests are sitting in the lounge, munching on the complimentary breakfast and sipping coffee, talking quietly.

My morning task the day of the wedding was to get the groom dressed. Well, to push him along. He showed up in our hotel room forty-five minutes later than we expected and I practically pushed him into the shower. Ultimately, and he agreed in hindsight, by getting done ahead of schedule, he had time to finish his speech, micro-manage some more, eat lunch and relax a little bit. The bride on the other hand, was late for her hair appointment and came back frazzled and rushed to get into her gown.

I was given the keys to the Durango (8 passenger) and carted four Ukrainians and three Spanish bridesmaids to the Church.

The Wedding Ceremony

It was a Catholic wedding in the Filipino traditions. An entirely pleasant hour spent among friends and Jesus. The ceremony went more or less the way it was supposed to. The deacon did his thing, though I tuned most of it out, and another friend of ours, Sherman (who doubled as the wedded couple's driver after the ceremony) read a prepared religious passage from the pulpit. It was all very pleasant and warm.

For those who aren't familiar with the Filipino wedding tradition, it involves lighting candles, wrapping a veil around the bride and groom and then knotting them together with a rosary. They also exchange coins (a precursor to the joint bank account apparently) and, of course, traditional Catholic wedding vows. The wedding party was huge. It included three bridesmaids, three groomsmen, a best man, a matron of honor, the parents and the principle and secondary sponsors. The latter, as I understand it, evolved from members of the community who essentially offered to support the couple in their earliest days of marriage by making large donations to the marital coffers. I don't know if there is an actual exchange of money in the modern interpretation, or if the role is more symbolic at this point. The wedded couple, towards the end of the ceremony, also went around and kissed and hugged each member of the wedding party.

Both the processional and the recessional had more of a mad-dash quality than a deliberate and rhythmic pattern. As one of the groomsmen, I can tell you straight up if there was music playing to pace our speed, I never heard it. I let my partner pace us anyway. I wasn't going to pretend I knew more than a brides-maid about the correct pace of walking down the aisle.

There was this flurry of exit, then a flurry of pictures. Sure, the bride and groom never had a shot of them getting into the car and driving away (mostly because the crowd of guests refused to cooperate with the photographer and became more of a wall than a door). I hear Sherman, who was ready to drive them off to blissful marriage in the Cadillac after the wedding, grumbling under his breath.

They overturned the church in about ten minutes for a 4pm mass. It was a slick operation.

From SmartReMarx.com
Wedding Tales: Reception Still March 25, 2006
Posted by Andrew

The reception hall was absolutely gorgeous. It was the design of an old English manor and they ushered the bridal party upstairs for photographs and munchies. Downstairs, they opened the cocktail hour thirty minutes ahead of schedule in order to accommodate guests who had arrived early. The cocktail hour hors d'oeuvres were exquisite. There was a little bit of everything from pasta to fish to stir fry to cheese nibbles and my personal favorite; deep fried yumminess. The room quickly filled up with too many people and I declared my intentions to sit outside.

Did I tell you about the weather that day? Maybe mid-thirties (I'm being optimistic here), overcast, a gray cold day. But they had warmers out on the deck and tables and what do you know? It was a pleasant improvement over being crammed into the tiny reception area with 155 other people and about seventy-five plates of millefeuille.

Given the personalities of the bride and groom, their need for control and order, it should not surprise anyone that the reception was actually more micromanaged than the ceremony. From the moment the crowd of well-wishing attendees entered the main dining hall and found their table assignments, every second of the next four hours was a carefully crafted and controlled environment to party.

I am going to go off on a tangent here and tell a story about my friends. The tables were designed to hold thirteen guests, not comfortably but securely. Nobody was meant to escape. The largest man at our table, we'll call him Sherman, sat at the end but we realized that we would have to break up a couple to keep him there. So he came around the table to losers' side and squeezed in between two of us. The result was an imbalance. In order to compensate and squeeze myself into a space that was not wide enough for me without slicing off one arm, I was practically sitting on the lap of the groomsmen on the other side of me. In order for either of us to get in and out of chairs, we had to both push off against the table, scooch our chairs backwards and away from each other, and then the departing person had to crawl on top of and over the other. It was more difficult to get seated (or rather, had we been sharing the same chair, we would have less difficulty with the arrangement). We were all so close, I think I caught an STD.

I suppose we had enough to drink that it really didn't matter. The only thing left was the wait for the dramatic grand entrance of the bride and groom and the real celebration was ready to start.

From SmartReMarx.com
Wedding Tales: At My Most Beautiful A Little While Later on
March 25, 2006
Posted by Andrew

To kick off the night, the bridal party was introduced. We fashioned a tunnel for the bride and groom to run underneath and then they began the first dance to At My Most Beautiful by R.E.M. FYI for all future wedders, you can't dance to this song. It has no beat, no discernable rhythm and it's too fast to slow dance to. I know, I know, it is the sentiment that counts. Just putting it out there.

I ordered the chicken. Oh yes, I got at least three "really? You ordered the chicken?" I mean, if the chicken wasn't a good choice, why was it on the menu? "Not the duck? I thought for sure you would order the duck." Fuck you, I ordered the chicken.

The dinner at the wedding reception was really good. The dancing music was salsa, I have nothing to say about that.

So look, that pretty much was the wedding in a nutshell. Except for two things: the speeches and the Jewish ceremony. In a way, I have nothing to comment about either. Both the father of the groom and the father of the bride gave very moving speeches. The matron of honor spoke at length about her devotion to her sister and the best man spoke on behalf of the groom. It was all very moving and appropriate.

The groom got up and gave a truly awesome speech, as a way of thanking the guests. He thanked each of the members of the bridal party individually and even gave part of the speech in some of the different native languages of the guests (English, Spanish, German, Ukranian, did I miss one?) It was really the only time I might have teared up. Normally a six page speech and I am out at the bar trying to plug my ears with slices of lime. And what do you know, six pages flew by.

As far as the Jewish ceremony, I really enjoyed that. The groom did all of the Hebrew portions and the bride translated into English. A lot of "lord our father, king of the universe" verses. The basic Jewish ceremony parts include Havdallah (on Saturday night, to conclude the Sabbath), the chupah (the traditional wedding canopy), the breaking of the glass. Last time I tried to explain this in any detail to someone, it got lost in translation. But it was a short service, it kept people engaged and I really thought it was excellently choreographed. The non-Jews could follow the gist. It was a nice touch to have a Catholic wedding and a Jewish ceremony to honor the traditions of the couple.

Speaking of food (trust me, we were) we also were treated to cleansing sorbet and the wedding cake (or another cake we were meant to believe was the wedding cake after they wheeled it out of the room! This conspiracy brought to you courtesy of the groom). I didn't really enjoy the wedding cake. I'm not a big fan of fruit stuffed into the interior of cake, and where was the frosting? I don't think you are supposed to bad mouth wedding cakes, it might be the height of poor manners. I never met a wedding cake that really worked it for me, but I feel like I have enough experience to speak on the matter.

But hey, maybe it's just me, but if that is the worst thing that happened that night, that's pretty good for a wedding, right?

The Sunday morning after was about goodbyes and farewells. When the hotel later asked me about my stay, my only real complaint was about the carb-overload at the complimentary continental breakfast. I know, it was free (well, included) but the thing is, we live in a world where you are only as gassy as your last meal.

I'm telling you, no matter what tale you're telling, it always comes back to food.

From Concert-Central.com
Calexico, Emo's, Austin, TX April 15, 2006
Review by Dara

Free acoustic show that we had to arrive two hours early for, buzz made it exciting but the show was quite good, they were a little weird to me, homey ... well acoustic I guess, bland lead singer with average voice, what was very special about them was their trumpets and the songs that were black Spanish magic.

From: Dara Shifrer
To: amarx
Subject: Pick Up the Receiver, I'll Make You a Believer
Date: Mon, 08 May 2006

(Sending last week's e-mail again b/c got a denial message)

Andy,

I do not know why it has taken me so long to respond to this e-mail! I look at it at home and at work and put it off to a more witty time. Not really feeling witty now - just unequipped currently to do anything else. Guess I'm not feeling witty very often at all lately. ;-) Things are hardly as ugly as I am implying - just too many allergies in the air and too much end-of-the-school-year frenzy.

I did a quick little search on Bennington and it is host to a sweet 35,000 residents!!!! That's the county of Bennington actually. Wow. On the plus side, "Bennington - Where Vermont Begins Welcome to Bennington, Vermont! A beautiful community nestled in the southern part of Vermont, Bennington is a great place to visit, and an even greater place to live." But it sounds like you didn't feel good about the job anyway. A pretty small town appeals to me on some levels but I don't fancy it for my current life. As you said, meeting people and having things to do... But I suppose the presence of the college creates some of those things. I don't know - maybe you would make better and deeper friendships. I'm not so busy but life is moving swiftly. Three weeks left of teaching...I want to say forever but who knows. Maybe after I rack up $40,000 in debt I'll return to my teaching position with that $1000/year pay raise. I'm really enjoying teaching but not regretting leaving it. Still an oddly stressless year - such small classes and fewer classes. I am writing curriculum this summer for one week - good way to leave and good way to enter education research. I told you I'm going to Belize for the month of June? I found a religion grad student from Rice to stay in my apartment for that month which is thrilling. We'll go to Guatemala for a few days before leaving the area. I am DEFINITELY coming to see you in Las Vegas. Julianna reports to me that you will actually be there all week rather than just Thu-Sun. Is that your and Becca's private time? I'll probably show up Thu/Fri anyway. Really looking forward to it actually. Michael is being very good to me which makes me scared that bad news is coming but that is definitely my issue. He's only been back a week and some days though. It is nice. Julianna is a mess of sick victimized woman mentality to the point that I can't abide talking to her about it. My mother exists in a daily litany of drama and misery. Which is somewhat verifiable but it always seems to me it could be approached with more optimism. Like what would she do with herself if there weren't drama? Drama only exists as much as you allow it too. I have made new girl friends in Austin. One actually. Good. All right. Send me the update on Bennington. Maybe you love your current job now.

Bye!Dara

From Concert-Central.com
Daniel Johnston, Waterloo Records, Austin, TX May 11, 2006
Review by Dara

Painful to watch and didn't like the aspect of making a spectacle of mental illness, but after all the conflicting reports regarding the authenticity of his eccentricity I was surprised at the simple musicability of his music, it was basic and repetitive but enjoyable, genius in its way - lyrics are the key I think, has been covered by Nirvana and others.

From: Andrew Marx
To: dshifrer
Subject: RE: Pick Up the Receiver, I'll Make You a Believer
Date: Fri, 12 May 2006

I'm not sure I've heard the "must be witty" requirement for responding to e-mail. I don't plan on saying anything witty herein, so you might want to read it when you are in a somber mood. (Or maybe it's like alcohol and it enhances whichever mood you're in? If you're happy, you're happier. If you're sad, you're sadder. If your tummy hurts, your tummy hurts-er).

Things are a little whack here too, but I'm just flowing along the tide. Let's spin the wheel of topics and see where we shall begin. (Spin, spin) Julianna ... work ... Becca ... Vegas ... Boys ... Boston ... Julianna ... work ... Becca ... Vegas ... Boys ... Boston ... Julianna ... work ...

Becca ... Vegas ...

Boys,

Boys it is. I spent this week in a rather lengthy training session and one guy was downright flirty. He kept doing that thing where you make a point, and then touch the hand of the person you are talking to, as if for emphasis. Maybe this is solely a gay thing, I don't know. Naturally I positioned my hand in such a place as he could easily reach it at the conclusion of each thought. (I would have put it in his lap if I could have gotten away with it, he was flirting that ferociously). Definitely my type, but not sure if he's single. 34, taller than me by a couple heads. He smokes, which I think is not a huge plus but for the purposes of harmless flirting, not particularly relevant. I'm not saying this is turning into anything, but it always fun to know guys like that.

Let's spin again, shall we?

Boston,

Well, I'm not moving to Bennington. One, I wasn't sold on small town living. I don't think it would have been the worst case scenario, but I had concerns. Two, the Dean I interviewed with thought I had a bad attitude. He said as much when he said, "I'm not sure you have the right attitude." So I wasn't terribly upset about the whole thing. The only real drawback to the entire interview process was the length of time, it was stretched out over three months. I would rather have condensed it into a couple of weeks.

But I might move back to Waltham. Right now, I live in the city, but it's not particularly cost efficient. If I can find a cheaper apartment, I will definitely move when my lease is up. Waltham has its quirks, but let's face it, it has become my home town for better or for worse, crazies and all. I just need to embrace my inner-Waltham and be done with it. Bonus, it is close to work. Bonus, all my friends live close by.

(Spin, spin)

I don't really have any topic related to Julianna and Becca. Julianna doesn't return my e-mails. So whatever. But clearly Julianna must be in contact with Becca, so that's interesting. Becca and I are going to Vegas from Monday to Monday but no, definitely NOT just our private time. Just a quirk of the schedule and vacation time. We'll fit in anyone who wants to join us during that time. I also have friends (as does she) in Vegas that I want to catch up with before the excitement of the weekend. I am going to get Becca to agree that we don't need to spend 24/7 with each other. Some vacations, that works better than others, but I definitely just want down time to wander the city or visit with people or whatever. That includes over the weekend. So that if (for example) you and I want private time, we just meet and send everyone else away. That week is very ambitious for me.

It's been raining for days and days here. Doesn't particularly bother me, but I do so love people's incessant need to analyze the weather. Aside from picking out weather-appropriate attire, I don't think most topics of conversation need to revolve around excessive rain/sunshine/snow/heat. I am in the minority. My mom says it is because it's a "safe" topic.

But how exciting for Guatemala. I have a friend who lives in Mexico. His father is a rich lawyer in New York and he basically rejected all that and became a student in sustainable development. Anyway, he worked in Guatemala and also Nicaragua for a few years, respectively. His stories were always very rich. I don't know anything about Belize however.

So, I'm glad you're coming to Vegas. Please be in touch before you leave for Belize so I know that your stress levels have come down a little. You sound like you're ready for the end of the semester, so I guess it's a good thing it's here.

AM

---- Original Message ----
From: Dara Shifrer
To: amarx
Subject: RE: Concert Site
Date: Tue, 10 Apr 2007

singer/songwriter for The Mountain Goats (to remind me)

From: Andrew Marx
To: dshifrer
Subject: RE: Concert Site
Date: Tue, 10 Apr 2007

John Darnielle or Peter Hughes - not sure if they write collaboratively or not. I'm downloading a couple of their tracks now.

From: Dara Shifrer
To: amarx
Subject: RE: Concert Site
Date: Tue, 10 Apr 2007

HA ha! No no! Can you add the subgenre 'Singer/Songwriter' under Rock or Soft Rock - though I appreciate the extra information. ;)

5

Chapter Five *Music Is My Boyfriend*

---- Original Message ----
From: Andrew Marx
To: dshifrer
Subject: On the Quick
Date: Thu, 8 Jun 2006

I don't remember when you are going on your trip to Belize, so maybe you already left. But in any case, I am now dating the boy. He's fun, very humorous, very sarcastic. He's more diplomatic than I am when it comes to his humor. Less pointing out others' inadequacies and more making fun of his own. His taste in music is pretty diverse, mostly stuff I have never heard of. But it's not bad. He's also into the Pretenders and Tom Petty and the like, and we overlap there.

I moved into a new office on campus, with a new job and many new responsibilities (in addition to the old ones). I am trying to land a new apartment that would get me closer to work and the boy and the landlord sort of nixed my application so I have an appointment with him at 1pm to talk him out of it. (Or rather, talk my way into the apartment). I can stay where I'm at but I hate the commute and all my friends live closer to work and the new apartment.

Vegas plans proceed apace. I found a restaurant for my birthday party. It's a tapas bar in Las Vegas near the Hard Rock Hotel. I floated this idea of doing a city-wide scavenger hunt with Becca. My friends who live there are coordinating the hunt, although I would have done it myself too. I guess you're not supposed to know in advance what items are on the list so you can't collect them in advance. (I'm not that dedicated to winning, or even betting to show). The idea could be fun, if executed properly.

---- Original Message ----
From: Dara Shifrer
To: undisclosed-recipients:;
Subject: A Mass Bulletin from Belize
Date: Sat, 17 Jun 2006

My life in the last three weeks has basically consisted of paper bags. 1000s of bags of ceramics, 1000s of bags of lithics (i.e. fancy rocks that are the center of Michael's existence) and a few bags of obsidian. Moving bags from a corner on the floor to a table to another table to a shelf to a box... Most of the bags have large elderly spiders and some have scorpions. After a student had to step outside and cry after her first scorpion sighting and other female students started refusing certain job duties from fear of the same, my sympathy with their female weakness was fast waning until I unfortunately ran into the biggest blackest scorpion EVER and screamed like a girl. To make up for it, I killed my first scorpion the very next day (never mind that it was 1/4 inch long). I've been bribing people to do my killing ever since.

The lab that houses the artifacts from the multitudes of archaeologists who have used this as their "camp" since 1991 was unorganized and frightening enough to bring me to tears in the first week (not to mention the collection of directors whose priorities were individually each of top importance). But despite not knowing archaeology, the Shifrer regimen in cleaning and organizing has held me in good stead. I'm even thinking about burning candles for a little atmosphere in there now. ;-)

Otherwise, camp life has reminded me of how young 19 years of age is. Not as different from middle school teaching as I previously thought. Lots of drama and intrigue and energy. There are steamy latrines, cold showers, beans at every meal and the conversation generally revolves around bug bites. The charm should endure for just about the four weeks that I am here. Hated to send a mass e-mail but I have had much less e-mail time than I expected. I wanted to let everyone know I was safe and having a good time! Hope that you are as well.

From: Dara Shifrer
To: amarx
Subject: RE: On the Quick
Date: Wed, 28 Jun 2006

Well, Andy, do tell!!! New boy AND new job responsibilities! The two cruxes of life. I don't recall you referring to your love life as "dating" very often, so I would definitely appreciate any details you are able to provide. It all sounds very serious if you are attempting to move closer to it all.

Did the landlord meeting work out?

So I have happily finished my sentence at the archaeology camp. It was a success on all levels. Work-wise, romantic-wise and health-wise, but I am happy to be finally and truly vacationing. We arrived in Antigua, Guatemala yesterday morning, and besides having access to e-mail, I have access to masses of ruined churches and the damn finest food I've had in many a day.

Regardless, I am looking forward to my return to some sort of normalcy (June 3rd) and also my trip to the Las Vegas extravaganza!! Maybe I won't recognize you? I'm getting the "it's time for dinner bitch" stare, so will tell more soon.

Dara

From Andrew Marx
To: dshifrer
Subject: One Man Guy
Date: Sun, 2 Jul 2006

Well, nothing ever works as smoothly as it sounds on paper.

There hasn't been a lot of "dating," just a lot of dates - the difference being multiple dates with the same guy. Hans and I have been "dating" for about five weeks now but we are still very early in the relationship. The other day, my friend Jeremy asked me if I saw a future with Hans. I adore Hans, but I was horrified about the question. I don't see the future, but I also kind of think that 5 weeks isn't that much time really to know someone. But Jeremy wasn't the only one who has sort of couched it like that. Can you possibly know after five weeks whether you want a future?

We are very different though, which amuses me more often than not. He's a hillbilly, truck-driving, beer-drinking pothead with a wicked sense of humor. I'm stuck up, conservative and up tight (oh yes, you heard it here first). He spends money without reservation, I calculate everything. He lives in the country (what passes for the sticks in Massachusetts). I live in the 'burbs. He's big on the outdoors, I put up with it.

I'm trying very hard not to over complicate things, but alas, I suck at it. I'm trying very hard to keep my crazy contained, and I suck at that too.

Assuming that we are still dating in another five weeks, maybe my prognostication skills will be better honed then...

As for the new position, so far the transition has been rough. I didn't think it would be; I thought this was a great opportunity. I just want to run and shove my head under the mattress and not come up for air. My goal is to make it another month. 1) I got vacation coming 2) The girl who is training me is leaving so I will be fully vested in the work responsibilities.

Plus, I'll be in the new apartment then, should have a small raise, and be a lot more grounded all the way around. Ask me then! Whatever the question was.

If you have a Vegas itinerary, can you please send it to me? Thank you.

See you soon.

Andy

From: Dara Shifrer
To: amarx
Subject: RE: One Man Guy
Date: Sun, 2 Jul 2006

Haaa ha haa. What is awry in this universe if you are dating the boys that I am supposed to date!?! You do sound very head over heels over this beer-swilling, pot-smoking hillbilly, even if the prospect of long-termity is terrifying you. Gosh, your e-mail made me smile. So please please me and send more details, like how-in-the-good-name-of-satan you met, and what he does and what you all do together? Well, what you do about town at least. ;-)

I am actually surprised to hear that there is crazy in you. I wouldn't suspect it. I assume you're talking jealous-making, crazy love crazy. Isn't it disturbing? To lose your equilibrium, self-control and self-sufficiency? I hate love most, well some, days. I just can't imagine this situation. Are you guys going HIKING together? Are you guys already talking about a future? Oh my.

That's how it was when I met Michael. It was so immediately apparent that we fit well - ridiculously easy to be together - we regularly marveled at it mid-date - and I went mad and agonized over our lack of potential for a future and made everything very difficult. And maybe it was all true, but ever since I gave up trying to figure out the future immediately, things have been very smooth.

So we have returned to "4-star" Princess Hotel in 0-star Belize City. 4 nights in Antigua - a lovely colonial city that is the least Latin American city in Guatemala. The restaurants are great, there are lots of nice hotels and nice shops...sometimes more Europeans/Americans than locals. We had a very nice time. I leave for Austin tomorrow evening. Michael is staying in Belize for one more week to present a paper at the Belize Symposium. He was notified in an untimely manner about his presentation so is having to make the vacation a working one. I am not disappointed to be going home. Bed, good showers, and my Crahobi.

My tentative itinerary for Vegas is the 23rd and 24th - I haven't planned lodging b/c I'm unsure if Michael will be with me. I don't think he will be, will solidify plans this week and notify you!

Thanks for the e-mail/hope the job has phased back into not-sucking-ass,

Dara

From: Andrew Marx
To: dshifrer
Subject: RE: One Man Guy
Date: Fri, 7 Jul 2006

I'm a little enamored with Hans, but having said that, we also are still in the 'just dating' phase so I don't want to put too much emphasis on it. I like that things are evolving naturally (or rather, in spite of my incessant anxiety which I keep carefully hidden from him).

So the story of how we started dating.

He bought me lunch one day during that week of training we were at. Which I thought was highly inappropriate at the time, him paying and all. So I went to Vermont that weekend with Becca and came back and was ill, ill, ill for days. Finally, feeling mostly depressed but no longer physically sick, I was chatting with my friend Josephine about Hans and feeling sorry for myself and whatever, and Josephine says, just e-mail him. So I did, and I said "I owe you a lunch." He said, how about tomorrow? We had lunch, it was great, he asked me out at the end of lunch and that is how it started.

It's raining big time again. I swear this has been the rainiest summer. Yesterday, it was torrential and I went out in shorts to pick up dinner (I'm moving next week so grocery shopping has been reduced to a minimum) and I got a few mosquito bites just in that ten minute window I was outside. It was nice though because it was very wet and very hot.

Vacation all I ever wanted...

AM

From: Dara Shifrer
To: amarx
Subject: The Itinerary
Date: Thu, 13 Jul 2006

Michael is coming with me. I am coming mid-week because the other main purpose of driving out there is to see my family which needs to happen on the weekend. We will stay in Vegas Wednesday and Thursday nights, July 26th and 27th. You, Becca and Julianna are the main people I want to see, though I may try to fit in a few stragglers. Will I be able to see you, oh, pretty please!?!

;-) Dara

From: Andrew Marx
To: dshifrer
Subject: RE: The Itinerary
Date: Thu, 13 Jul 2006

Becca and I have a show Wednesday night, but it's not until 10:30pm at night. We can do dinner beforehand. Any time on Thursday is yours if you like. If you are so inclined, we are going to midnight breakfast at Orleans on Friday around 12:01

am (so Thursday night). Wednesday afternoon is good too. Just say when.

What's Julianna got to do with it? I haven't heard from her in six months. She never responded to any e-mail or phone call from me since she moved, and as far I can tell, she keeps telling you and Becca that she's interested in coming. Which is great, but don't you think she could be bothered to mention it to me?

From: Dara Shifrer
To: amarx
Subject: RE: The Itinerary
Date: Sun, 16 Jul 2006

Andy,

So though this has all been confirmed with your secretary, Becca, I thought I'd inform you as well so as not to incur the rath that Julianna has earned. ;-)

Our dates changed to the nights of 25th and 26th - not too big a change and good news for us b/c Michael's parents gave us two nights at a homestay they have in Vegas. We are hoping to at least have dinner with you guys (and I guess Marie as well?) on Wednesday the 26th. I was trying to get excited about a restaurant but I just didn't eat out in Vegas enough to know any. Becca brought up Tito's and I brought up Battista's... I would love to try your sushi place (never have) but I believe Michael is not a sushi fan.

Becca reports that you are still seeing Hans - we are both disappointed that he is not coming to Vegas but it is understandably
"too soon." I LOVE how you met. His sweet bold gesture and
your volley back in the same.

Really looking forward to seeing you,

Dara

From: Andrew Marx
To: dshifrer
Subject: RE: The Itinerary
Date: Mon, 17 Jul 2006

Hans definitely will not be coming along. As it is, I think the
dating thing has already stalled, reasons unknown. To me at
least. Currently we still e-mail 3 times a day, but there is no
steaminess in the off hours and now that I think about it, maybe
the e-mail frequency is one-sided at that. Plenty of time for bit-
terness and recrimination after Vegas, if that becomes necessary!

Becca called me with your basic information. She's so funny.
She thinks she's running interference with you. Ah well, at this
point, you are probably right, I won't be speaking to Julianna
until I have to. She told Becca she was still thinking of coming,
but I just can only shrug my shoulders and soldier on.

My friend Marie loathes sushi, so I know how it is to work with
those types. Friday night's sushi dinner will be pretty small; just

five or six of us. Marie's the only one I'm worried about, but hey, there's a Carl Jr. or something on every block.

I'll let you and Becca sweat the details of our rendezvous. Why else have a press secretary if she doesn't represent?

From ~~SmartReMarx.com~~ *No matching record was found*
The Previously Untold Story of Blog Vegas IV August 2, 2006
Posted by Andrew

I used to write a Blog Vegas diary for every trip back to the motherland, but this year's trip diary was never published and the pages were subsequently shredded and later burned and finally buried in a secret location known only to me, the grave-digger and Captain Jack.

I'm not gonna lie. There were some personality conflicts. (I'm being generous.) There's no way to tell the story without hurting someone's feelings. That, of course, is why I burned all the documentation. Out of respect for the fact that there are two sides to this story. One in which someone else is the evil bitch, and one in which I am. I, of course, have witnesses, but I shall never call them to court, never swear them under oath to any version of the story which makes me appear to be respectable, nay, generous of heart and wallet. But should they deign to tell their versions of the story, and should it turn out in their versions that I, in fact, was restrained in my behavior and magnanimous to a fault, neither shall I dispute the account nor prevent them from offering it.

From Concert-Central.com
The Meteors, Emo's, Austin, TX August 12, 2006
Review by Dara

OTMAPP = Only the Meteors Are Pure Psychobilly (this is what people chant at their shows), the first psychobilly say they though The Cramps were contemporaneous, they were much more popular in the UK, Rockboy was very excited, they were hard for sure and driving and that's the end of their goodness, no diversity in the music and no show, they apparently do not throw up blood any longer

From: Dara Shifrer
To: amarx
Subject: Of Trivialities
Date: Mon, 14 Aug 2006

What's up snuggle-butt? I hear through the gossip mill that you and Marie skipped out on your Las Vegas birthday dinner. They said that you were sick. I suspect you were sick of people, but if I am mistaken, I hope that you're feeling better. How was the week? What all did you and Becca do? See anybody interesting?

The Apple Valley visit was pretty excellent insofar as visits home go. Hectic and loud and frantic but that is to be expected. I don't think Michael would wax as positive as I though. We did have a great trip until the drive home when living together was discussed and he basically would not respond except for placidly farting at me. Not a pretty scene.

I have been working some three jobs since returning. Tutoring, typing and temping. In good news, my future professor advisor finally came through and found me work on their research project. So tomorrow I meet them at 10:30am. I'm basically cleaning up little messes that they have been stacking in a corner. I gather that it may involve modifying their website which is definitely not something I have any experience in. But it is too good of an opportunity for me to quibble.

How is your new beau? How is the job? How is Boston?

Dara

From: Andrew Marx
To: dshifrer
Subject: RE: Of Trivialities
Date: Mon, 14 Aug 2006

What I told Becca on that Saturday was that I wasn't feeling it. She chose to accept that as canceling the party due to illness, but the girl is not stupid and simply utilized the easiest explanation. What happened was, among other things, a number of birthday party guests had to cancel last minute due to family emergency and whatnot and by Friday, we were already heading to the party with substantially less people than the RSVP.

So then on Saturday, when the party was actually scheduled for, I get wind of the fact that Becca has somehow managed to invite five or six friends to my birthday party and she expected me to treat them. So by canceling, I was obligating *her* to treat them seeing as how they were now expecting a free meal. Now, I knew three of the people she had invited, and okay fine, they weren't all strangers but why am I spending $600 on a birthday party when the ratio of my friends to Becca's friends is, at the very best, 1:1?

But keep in mind that was Saturday. Now let's rewind:

Becca and I barely managed to maintain civility during the trip (mostly by ignoring each other) but it started early, on Monday, when Becca began the day with a litany of complaints against my decision making. It got bad, really really bad. First it was we woke too early (my fault), got to the airport too early (again, my fault), checked in to the hotel too early (somehow my fault) and that was just by 2pm on day one! I didn't realize it was a preview of the whole trip! She went ballistic when I wanted to take a nap in the late afternoon and that's when I told her to fuck off. On day one.

The nap thing got way out of control. She kept making nasty comments about how I don't know "how to take vacation" and was I going to watch TV while in my hotel room because no one goes on vacation and *plans* to watch TV. Oh yeah. Added to the fact that she had plans to spend that night with some of her friends, so what did it really matter what I did? AND THE NEXT DAY, we spent hours going from 99cent store to 99cent store. She spent easily $50 every time and went back on her own later. Who does THAT on vacation?

Things got worse when Marie arrived from Boston on Wednesday. Becca admitted she was jealous that Marie and I had a better friendship than she and I, and then she decided to take it out on us for the rest of the week. Of course, we all went to dinner and things hadn't built up to incredulous points quite yet. The three of us then went to *Jubilee* that night. A topless extravaganza. Great show. Campy and entertaining. I have never seen so many boobs in my life. Definitely the boobies were a highlight of the trip. It's a classic Strip show (not strip, but The Strip) which are a dying breed so I wanted to see one while they are still around. We had front row seats, so we got showered with glitter and remnants of feather boas and the fake fog that rolls off the stage during the gymnasts' act. The costumes were wild with this enormous headwear and yes, some moments of scantily-cladness. The guys too. Up close like that, you can tell who waxes and who didn't make their last appointment. They had acrobatists and jugglists and a pair of twins who inserted themselves into tubing. (Oh, it's exactly as it sounds.)

By Friday, Becca and I weren't speaking. By Saturday, Marie was basically vowing to never speak to or be around Becca again.

It turns out nobody was excited about the scavenger hunt except Becca. I had to have a long talk with Becca about the appropriateness of this "competition". I tried to say, it's for fun, it's not serious, it's so that people can explore parts of Vegas. It was a nightmare. Forget the fact that it was designed for us to drive 25 miles all over town, the "items" were hard. I mean, you had to guess what you were actually looking for and it was so not fun. I said to Becca before we got into our respective cars, "These are really hard items, you know?" She looks at me, says "This is the way scavenger hunts are supposed to be." Not in my world. In my world, they involve a lot more margaritas.

She did end up treating her peeps to some dinner that night, while I went with my own friends to a casino somewhere out towards Blue Diamond and we spent the night rockin' the slot machines. I don't remember what we had for dinner, but I'm quite sure we each paid for our own meals.

Sunday was tense and ended with a row between Becca and I over tickets to go to the top of the Stratosphere. Marie had passed on going up to the observation deck so I got in line to buy just two tickets. By the time I got them, Becca had backed out of going with me (not that she mentioned anything until after I had spent the $30) and furthermore, "offered" for lend me her camera so I could take pictures for her. I graciously let them both walk off into the casino, and then I handed the tickets over to a couple of college students and stormed out.

On Monday after we had checked out of the hotel, Marie and I suggested seeing a movie at the Red Rock Station movie theater in the early afternoon. Becca seemed okay with the idea (we had hours to kill and neither of us wanted to spend the time talking to her) and we LET HER PICK THE MOVIE. Later that night, at dinner, she tells us that she would never have gone to see a movie because she has to sit all night on the red eye and she didn't need to be sitting for an additional two hours just beforehand. Our flight was at 11:30 at night. Not to mention I see no discernable difference between sitting at a slot machine for two hours and sitting in a movie theater. It was ludicrous that she would even think it, much less say it out loud.

She attributed the ruin of her vacation to me, openly I might add. I'm not overdramatizing anything. Because I couldn't stick to a schedule, Marie couldn't make a decision and we were both lethargic and wanted to spend the whole time in our hotel rooms. Direct quote, I'm not making this up.

The time off was necessary. The rest of it? I don't know what to think. Becca is going to deny everything of course, so I'm not sure at what point it's even worth talking to her about it. She complained constantly, she was argumentative during 90% of any conversation. You know, she was furious at Julianna for deciding to come last minute and then not making any time to spend with us. My response was, we do what we do, and if Julianna wants to join us, then great. If not, no big deal. Oh that really pissed her off. Because at that point, now I'm not doing anything to admonish Julianna for her rude behavior (now, come on, this is Julianna. What good would that have done?) AND I'm not helping to plan our own time to hang out with her. Everything was such an ordeal. It was unreal.

So the problem is that I don't have a sense of humor about it. I wasn't particularly miserable. If nothing else, Becca gave me a lot to gossip about during the trip. But now I don't know what to make of it. It doesn't make me laugh; I'll tell you that much.

So different topic:
I liked Michael. He has that sort of "I'm better than you are" thing going, but he passes it off well. How is your relationship going?

Oh, and Hans and I broke up the same day I got back from Vegas. It was a long time coming. No reason given. We didn't even really break up, so much as simply stopped dating. Breaking up implies drama.

The conversation went like this:

Me: So are we still dating? Because, you know, we don't go on dates? Him: It did kind of fizzle out, didn't it? Are we still going out on Friday? Let's talk about it then.
Me: Um...
(At this point, my Vegas luggage is on the doorstep of the apartment and he comes over and gives me a hug exactly like someone had died).

As a postscript, he stood me up on Friday.

Job woes are another e-mail.

Andy

From: Dara Shifrer
To: amarx
Subject: Music Is My Boyfriend
Date: Tue, 15 Aug 2006

What a piece of juicy gossipy goodness!! That was a candy e-mail for sure. You clearly have been pent-up with it to have unleashed at such length.

While I enjoy my few hours with Becca - I can trust her to immediately launch into detailed updates with Becca-perspective asides about anyone and everyone in our acquaintance - I do not put any of the described behavior past her. She has a history, a very long history, of occasional negativity and nitpickiness. The girl is so persistent and doesn't seem to know how to dig her way out of things. I guess everybody struggles to be happy.

And no more Hans - I am sorry for that - though it sounds like it was a worthwhile experience to have had. Nowhere to go but up. And that will teach you to try to have fun for your birthday - tsk, tsk. ;-)

I am heading out in a moment to meet with my flaky professor and I just don't want to... because she's a flake. I'd rather be home working on scrapbooks and watching Fanny and Alexander. I just rented the monolith series - it was made by Ingmar Bergman and is very entertaining and wintery. Perfect escape from the unceasing Austin heat.

I have a cough. I'm sure my upstairs neighbor hates me. I coughed so much this morning I choked on my coughs and threw up a little in my hand. The sad truth. It's been going on like this for a week and so I finally went to the doctor yesterday and we decided I had been prescribed the wrong allergy medicine near a year ago and then she went and prescribed for the wrong symptoms again. Doctors that don't listen infuriate me.

Your summation of Michael was perfect and hilarious - even he smirked because he knew it was true. I am not sure, though, that it "works for him." I thought you guys might get on - you share some traits — a hatred for the majority of humanity - a refusal to subvert yourself. I'm having trouble phrasing those properly, but I mean them as compliments.

Bye!

Dara

From: Andrew Marx
To: dshifrer
Subject: RE: Music Is My Boyfriend
Date: Tue, 15 Aug 2006

I don't feel anything about the situation with Becca. Just disappointed. However, you of all people do understand, so I figured giving you the full story was worth it. Besides being a little bitter, Becca's problem has always been an inability to understand how other people perceive her. She always assumes what she thinks she's projecting (attitude, accomplishment, ethic) is what people internalize about her. Which as we well know, is far from what usually happens. Lesson from Vegas: Don't take the same flight out and back as anyone else in your party.

The plan now is just to keep the relationship to phone calls for the time being. I guess I'll deal with the long term ramifications later. She got me an ugly birthday gift, I hate to say. Marie and I were shopping in the Grand Canyon gift shops (complete with hourly thunderstorms if you can believe it) and I pointed out an ugly ugly trivet with an embossed image of the Las Vegas Welcome sign. When I opened my birthday gift from Becca, suddenly I owned the ugly trivet. I'm thinking of getting some adhesive and putting it up on the window pane like a stained glass. (P.S., the first time it got wet, it rusted).

All of which doesn't excuse her behavior, but she has earned a lot of latitude with me and we'll see where the future takes us.

I am inexcusably poor. That is what Vegas has wrought me. Lesson from Vegas: Start saving, and start saving early. Don't get me wrong, I spent perfectly within my budget on the trip, but I also just spent $3000 on moving costs and it all just seems like I'm back to struggling again. Oh the decisions we make. You're probably right, there's no where to go but up. Lesson from Vegas: Drink more, gamble while intoxicated. A piña colada before bed every night.

And I still have my actual birthday coming up. Have no idea the flavor of it, but I shall have to come up with something life changing to mark the occasion.

Over and out,

Andy

From Concert-Central.com
Long Shadows, Beerland, Austin, TX August 22, 2006
Review by Dara

Fantastic dark country, noodling like a spaghetti western, actually casting long shadows on the wall behind them, no vocals, prog to me but surf guitar to Rockboy, really liked them.

From: Dara Shifrer
To: amarx
Subject: And You Smell Like a Monkey Too
Date: Wed, 30 Aug 2006

Happy birthday to you.
Happy birthday to you.
HaapppPPPPPPYYYYY BBBBBBIRRRRRRRRRR
THDAAAAAAAY DEAAR ANNNNNNNNDYY!!!!!!
Happy birthday to you.

From: Dara Shifrer
To: amarx
Subject: RE: Music Is My Boyfriend
Date: Sat, 2 Sep 2006

Andy,

Well, hopefully your wealth has re-stabilized. I think your life lessons were excellent and will be drinking a piña colada before bed every night myself. I know a girl whose parents live in Florida and they do that very thing. They go down to their basement garden porch and actually pull a coconut out of the fridge, crack it open and have real coconut milk in their drinks. I thought it was an excellent way to live.

I've spent the last two weeks frantically working for my professor and getting ready to start school. School has actually started but I've only attended two classes and the class I'm TAing. It feels decadent to be idling in classrooms listening to professors drone on. I love it and feel guilty. They are all aimless drop-outs but maybe that's always been my goal?

I am currently in Atlanta, Georgia at the moment to be a brides-maid for my ex-Austin friend, Caecee. That aspect of the experience has been very egh (four nights here... eh), but last night they had a bachelor/bachelorette party at a campy strip club where the strippers are 50 years old plus and generally crazy.

The strip club was fantastic. Far nastier and campier than anything that I saw in Las Vegas. Total nudity and total proximity - you could catch a disease. The strippers kept up a string of crazy hilarious conversation in old-lady-smoker voices for the duration of the lap dances.

Les got his face slapped with breasts several times during one long lap dance - and she told him he was lucky that she was being gentle, lucky not to be getting a black eye.

The fifty-something year old in the Swedish girl dress, Portia, did smash beer cans between her breasts, longways and sideways. She told Caecee that her breasts happened to be perfect for can-smashing too, but to start off longways first or risk cuts - she kept muttering that it took her 12 years to figure that out. After she'd smashed a few cans, she reapplied her lipstick and kissed one can and presented it to Les - "Put it on your mantle."

The black lady with long golden curls finished off the couple's lap dance congratulating Les for getting a lady with a big ass and started singing "I like big butts and I cannot lie..." - Caecee was not pleased.

The nurse with stomach rolls and an exposed red bra put shots in the tube glass between her uncovered breasts for several people in the group - after they had it in their mouths, head upturned to swallow it (no hands), she would take the other end in her mouth and give it head.

And all of the strippers would turn around and grind the lap of the lap dancee - without any panties for protection. They all flashed their stuffon a regular basis - "red snapper," "peach cobbler," etc.

They all acted like they were just perverted children entertaining us - and there were a lot that seemed to be former men. Dressing room was IN the bathroom. I got a koozy."

In other points of interest, Les is Jewish and Caecee was a soul-seeking Christian who had been raised Atheist. She divorced her husband of four years in Austin, had a miserable time dating other guys in Austin and moved back home to Atlanta to end up meeting Les who would not be with her because she was not Jewish. Naturally, she converted. And I found myself at a mikva (?) on Friday morning. It was very very interesting. Foreign to me. She has, of course, embraced the traditions more than old-hand Les. They are currently at a service saying the blessings in tribute to their Sunday wedding - very very hungover. I am not hungover, because I am old and wise, and so I am going to go sit on their nice wooded porch and get work done. Hope you are happy and well.

Your friend,

Dara

From: Andrew Marx
To: dshifrer
Subject: It Is
Date: Fri, 8 Sep 2006

I have no idea what to do with your stripper story. In fact, I read it several times before I figured out that Les was the groom to be.

I am listening to Sarah McLachlan. I love her one album. It soothes me. Work is busy, but nothing newsy.

Later,

AM

From: Dara Shifrer
To: amarx
Subject: RE: It Is
Date: Wed, 13 Sep 2006

I am currently swimming in reading material and that pretty much sums up current life, there are no more spare moments, every moment is a potential reading moment. But, I love it and do not find it stressful in the daily way that teaching was. It's all interesting and stimulating as of right now. I guess I don't have a lot of confidence in my ability to be interested long-term. I will do my best as that is all I can do!

Life feels very good right now in all. Meeting new friends. Talking to adults. Liking Michael very much. Being challenged by school. I love that my schedule is all upside down, I can stay up late now, I can run in the morning. It's not this drudgery of sameness every day. Today is my long day - 10am til 9pm - with only 1/2 hour and hour-long breaks here and there. But the rest of the week is definitely not like that.

I am definitely not listening to Sarah McLachlan right now though I think Michael has a fondness for her - and my 22 year old sister. I like her Ice Cream song actually so I shouldn't be so rude in my thoughts toward her. I'm listening to Of Montreal "...we made love like a pair of black wizards . . . you fuck the suburbs out of me . . ." Mmmm...delicious.

Dara

From: Andrew Marx
To: dshifrer
Subject: RE: It Is
Date: Wed, 13 Sep 2006

I'm turned on to Of Montreal, but never added them to my cd collection. I heard about them ages ago, I can't remember through whom. Maybe you.

Talked to Julianna extensively about the Vegas trip. She had only heard snippets of the story from Becca and Marie (separately of course, and hardly the same version at that). Julianna's response was typically violent along the lines of "Becca can grow up," and "You should have said to her, 'My mother's name is [insert mother's name], she lives in [insert location]. I don't need another."

I do expect some way or another, Julianna will convey some part of that conversation to Becca, but since I'm not obliged to talk about it, I guess if Becca wants the lowdown, that's one way to get it. Life without Becca is going fine right now, so I'm not feeling pressured or sentimental to contact her. Not that she's out of my life completely, I don't usually act on sweeping declarative pronouncements. But not feeling pressured to remind her to take care of herself is actually liberating in a way.

Work is crazed, but it's not in a bad way. It's just I work in an office full of crazies and they really don't see it. They don't realize how complicated they make their own lives. But it amuses, and as long as it does so...

Love,

Andy

From: Dara Shifrer
To: amarx
Subject: RE: It Is
Date: Tue, 19 Sep 2006

Andy,

Ha ha ha! Your description of Julianna's part in your conversation was such classic Julianna. I could hear her dear voice cranking out those old lady bitterisms. She channels her mother more and more. I haven't spoken to her in weeks. She acts angry at me for not calling her, but then never has her phone on when I do call. It's very suspicious.

I'm surprised that you spent time telling Becca to take care of herself. I rather positioned your relationship the other way around, but maybe it is more symbiotic (I mean that word positively, I shouldn't be using a word I don't remember the definition of) than I think. I suspect that the two of you will talk again. I do believe that there is something to be said for longevity. We fight with those we love best, right?

I am a tiny bit crazed. I love the work but feel like the other parts of my life are not being tended to properly, which is probably because they aren't. I feel severely annoyed with Michael for no good reason, except maybe that he is not as busy as me. I've been cursing him all day as a slacker but maybe I'm just a workaholic. I used to viciously call him a workaholic. You're so smart to not date women.

The only stories that I can think to tell you involve the people in my cohort (forced friendships that I am happily taking advantage of) and reading reading reading. Durkheim, Marx and articles articles articles.

Tell me something funny,

Dara

From SmartReMarx.com
Loose on the Streets
Posted by Andrew October 1, 2006

Watch out, Waltham, I have wheels!

Ahem, that is, my friend went out of town and left me the keys to the car. Ah, the first time you sit behind the wheel again after months of spinning your wheels as a lower class pedestrian in suburban jail. Gripping the steering wheel and depressing the brake, hearing the click of gears when you put the car into reverse. Cranking up the stereo, hoping for "London Bridge" and settling for "Summer of '69." Hey, I didn't pick the station.

I was cautious for the first forty seconds of the drive. The time that it took to pull out of the driveway into actual, moving afternoon traffic. My heart fluttered with anticipation as the car roared and I plunged forward into my first intersection. Finally, I know what Bobby Labonte feels. And he only gets to drive around in circles.

I momentarily forgot my new freedom as I noticed what I had forgotten about driving in Waltham. Namely, the peculiar craziness that Waltham drivers bring to the game. I noticed a line of three cars driving in the median down High St. To be sure, they had their own lane, no need to inch even a quarter of the way into mine.

I hesitate to attribute all of the insanity to Waltham drivers because a lot of their driving idiosyncrasies are attributable to Massachusetts drivers in general. For instance, Mass drivers will cruise into right and left turns without any regard for oncoming traffic, the color of the traffic lights, or the weather. It's snowing, it's a red light, that means go. It's an unprotected left turn, it's rush hour, that means go. It's a right turn-only lane, but I'm going straight, that means go. Lanes are merging, and you're slowing down, that means go. It's a rotary, and traffic is at a dead stop, that means go.

Waltham has a particular dynamic between cars and pedestrians that is a direct result of the vast number of people who have nothing better to do than cross Moody St. back and forth all day, playing frogger with the privileged class of Waltham residents that drive. The trick is to get as many cars in one direction of traffic to come to a halt waiting for you to cross. Bonus points are awarded if you stop traffic at an intersection. Double points for causing a car going twice the speed limit to come to a screeching halt so that you can cross in front of them.

Now fold into the mix the commuter rail train that roars through Waltham station some fifteen times a day, an active bus depot, and a town full of college students and driving through Waltham to the highway can be an adrenaline rush. Now put me behind the wheel for the first time since I moved out of the suburbs, and get the hell out of the way.

Other towns have their quirks too. Everything stops for a funeral in Watertown. Newton, the snooty neighbor, their roads collapse down to one lane for both directions because of residents exercising their city-given rights to park any where they damn well please. Jamaica Plain, carefully protected against ground invasion because there is no way in and no way out. And Natick, where if you want to turn around, you have to drive to Framingham.

In fact, on my way to Natick by way of the Mass Turnpike, I still have to get to the highway. On the way there I encounter a pickup trying to back out of one driveway only to pull into the next driveway and park again. A Toyota driving dead in the middle of two lanes. And the notorious Route 20/ Highway 95 rotary.

The fact that I am out of gas. The fact that the car rumbles with an unfamiliar feel. The fact that the car in front of me is weaving between two lanes like a stumbling drunk. Nothing can dampen the euphoric feeling of being a driver once again. Time has eroded my caution and exhausted my driving instincts. All I know is that the highway ahead of me is clear, and Waltham now sits directly behind me flashing its pearly brilliance in my rearview mirror. I am freed from the suburban grip and on the highway, and that means go!

What Do You Say to the DJ?
by Andrew Marx and Dara Shifrer

a slightly phonographic tale

saytothedj.com

DING ALONG   TW 10/08

143

---- Original Message ----
From: Andrew Marx
To: dshifrer
Subject: Switch
Date: Tue, 16 September 2006

Dara, this is the text of the e-mail that I sent to Julianna:

"The truth of the matter is, Julianna, is that it is rare to meet a person who compliments you 100% in any relationship. The people we like best, we ignore the 10% or so that just is completely incompatible and accept the rest. I think a lot of couplings are closer to 50% compatible and 50% so not worth it, but people settle - they want love, or it's a good financial decision, or someone gets pregnant, or they have a string of unhealthy relationships and they have to lower standards. The thing is, 50/50 isn't really a bad thing - we do it in friendships, relationships with our parents (well, in my case, it's about 10/90 with my dad) but it helps to be objective enough, just long enough, to recognize where you are at in a given relationship.

Mind you, not everyone can be at all objective, and some people simply don't care to look that deeply. The great and tragic thing about all humans is that we all carry around emotional and mental baggage and it colors our perspective and the decision making process. We are a few pieces of puzzle and we fit well with some and we don't fit so well with others. Life is by far too fluid and unpredictable to spend an inordinate amount of time focused on your non-existent relationship to one person. Someone who clearly is not focused on you. So you have to decide, torture myself further, or do whatever I can do to get over this. Obviously, I suggest the latter if that is helpful to you to achieve a better sense of self, become whole again, be able to appreciate and enjoy the world around you. As adults, we come to the day when we can spend the rest of our lives being miserable about all the things we can't change, or we focus on the thing we CAN change and the rest happens as it happens.

I'm not saying it's easy for me to make the switch. I have to remind myself that some things are simply out of my control. Now, I believe philosophically, that we short change our potential by thinking TOO many things are out of our control when in fact, they are not. But generally, there is a laundry list of circumstances that each of us individually cannot affect the outcome of.

The side note to all of that is that humans also by nature are creatures of habit, and that very early on in our emotional and mental development, we establish patterns of behavior that are idiosyncratic and burned into our system - most people can't escape them. Sometimes they manifest as addictions, mostly habitual behaviors and attitudes that the inability to identify is ruinous. However, once you identify the patterns of behavior, it's still really hard to change and thus we live our lives in perpetual unending themes that cyclically repeat themselves until death departure. But in order to eschew the patterns of behavior, it takes force of will. That means there has to be desire on the part of the individual, effort and reinforcement. Some people don't get past the first step.

Stop sweating the small things, my dear.

Andrew"

6

Chapter Six *Sing-A-Long*

From *Concert-Central.com*
Wanda Jackson, Continental Club, Austin, TX October 20, 2006
Review by Dara

Did not want to go see some old lady doing early rockabilly but how could I not love her? Tiny spunky 70 year old. Clear that she'd lived but still had the restraint of an older generation. Voice is an awesome blend of raw scratch and melody. Knew how to bring the party. She created an experience. Must mention that she dated Elvis Presley, though he wasn't the husband helping her off the stage.

---- Original Message ----
From: Dara Shifrer
To: amarx
Subject: Stop sweating the small things
Date: Mon, 30 Oct 2006

I have decided that sociology is fairly depressing. I enjoy a good issues talk annnny day, but day in, day out, power struggles and inequality. The world is a pit of misery and despair, and it has been always. And if you are getting any enjoyment, it is very likely at the expense of some other unlucky soul. It's all hopeless of course.

I am to write a 25 page paper analyzing Durkheim and Weber's views on religion (do you know them?). And the only thing I have really discovered is how much of my life perspective is due to being raised Catholic. And that working hard is a bullshit Puritanical invention. I wrote a 24 page paper yesterday (supposed to be 8 so I'm in big trouble) on the whiteness of education in America.

I spend more time in coffee shops that I ever have in my life and it's just delightful. Austin, I guess unsurprisingly, has a kick ass coffee shop scene. Much more pleasant to work hours upon hours with other people doing the same. Interesting music, better tables than I have at home. Some winking over the tops of the computers.

I just saw The Importance of Being Earnest by Oscar Wilde for the first time - it is a criterion movie. I think you might like it - all about sharp wit, sarcasm and not being earnest. Also saw the Tao of Steve, which was funny and entertaining. He uses Buddhist philosophy to lay women.

I have all of this time because I stopped speaking to Michael on Friday night. We have an excellent time together and I see him most every night, but he doesn't want me to spend the night as often as I would like and won't progress things otherwise (move in together). He mocks disabilities and excuses, but is basically claiming emotional disability - he "retreats" when I bring up difficult subjects and just "can't give all of himself." Luckily, I am still furious enough (cumulative effect) to not be sad and to be getting things done that have needed to be done for some time.

I saw The Mountain Goats last night. It was quite the most entertaining show that I have seen in a long time. I don't know if you know them. It's very off kilter literate singer/songwriter music. The lyrics are striking, bizarre and funny. They're a little bit understated so I was worried it might be dull, but the singer was just as bizarre in person. Eyes pushed into his nose and crazy faces of repressed insanity as he sang in near whispers. Songs with the most minimal guitar you ever heard. One of their songs is "The Best Ever Death Metal Band Out Of Denton," and you can't comprehend the hilarity of that unless you hear the pleading dorky way it is sung and know that Denton is this tiny Texas town with a thriving jazz scene only b/c of a college there.

I must report to TA duty.

Happy Monday to you,

Dara

From *Concert-Central.com*
The Mountain Goats, The Parish, Austin, TX October 29, 2006
Review by Dara

I LOVED this show, the most minimal guitars you've ever heard (at times) and a totally unpredictable voice which all fit with their studio work. The surprise was the dynamism of Mike - he was all repressed insanity - face contortions while he sang a ballad. Great lyrics and then these monologues in between each song that were Hilarious. He came off as this tortured smart ex-gothic (eyes very close together) who was saved by this band. And when the guitars stopped being minimal all three of the boys played well, one guy did keyboards at times. So interesting and bizarre in a not very loud way.

From: Andrew Marx
To: dshifrer
Subject: RE: Stop sweating the small things
Date: Mon, 30 Oct 2006

Precisely because I have nothing better to do with my time:

http://www.nanowrimo.org/

This seems like something right up your alley, in a different year. They also raise money for libraries in Vietnam and the Congo, but somehow that doesn't excite me much as a fundraising opportunity.

Work is fine. The atmosphere doesn't thrill me but I like the kind of work I do (except for the leftovers from my old job) so I guess it will keep for now. I'm planning my grand move from Boston, years away, but much closer now. I'm just conflicted on where I want to end up. California is out. Las Vegas is probably a bad idea. How long is your graduate program? Have you thought about what comes after? (If I just made you cry, then forget I asked. I've had those days).

I think the world is a cesspool. It is so damnably hard to find positive inertia, it's scary. It scares me to think that people eagerly raise kids in this world and I just hope they don't impart all their negativity and prejudice and anger on to those poor children.

Sometimes I think you just have to shake things up. You've been doing pretty well at that lately. The thing about Michael, and boys in general, is that we tend to find someone that makes us feel good but for some reason, circumstance doesn't allow it to be a lasting relationship. But the thing is, we all feel like we need the constant validation to keep going. Maybe we do, but you know that given another set of circumstances, there is another boy out there for you. Well, I don't know if that makes you feel better, it was sort of intended to.

I liked my last one a lot, a lot, but circumstances just weren't happening. Hans cited depression and anxiety and a history of shitty relationships and I'm like, "Live in the present, jackass!" I'm afraid I was unnecessarily harsh in my last couple of e-mails to him, and even going back and reading them again makes me cringe. Sadly, I don't feel like we dated long enough for it to have caused quite this much drama in the fall out. Though come to think of it, that's how all of my so-called relationships have worked out. He was fuckin' adorable though, and I can finally admit I'm attracted to the smoking-like-a-chimney type.

Over and out,

AM

From Concert-Central.com
The Slits, Emo's, Austin, TX November 11, 2006
Review by Dara

Maybe my favorite show ever. They were so excellent I take a deep breath now. British inflected reggae. Stupid crazy outfits - party girls but not "typical girls." Then some punk. I do have a soft spot for girl rockers but these girls crafted such fine fine songs.

From: Dara Shifrer
To: amarx
Subject: Better love next time, baby. - Dr. Hook
Date: Tue, 14 November 2006

You are not the only one who offered me a spot in the writing marathon, but you ARE the only one who had the insight to recognize that additional writing in this first semester is about the last thing ... I do think it's a charming idea. I've been toying with the idea of advertising myself on match.com, just to jolt me out of the funk and make me date. But narrowing myself into pat little categories and describing "what I want" is inexpressibly depressing to me right now. I can't bring myself to create a MySpace account either, and some days I really want to. I just can't decide if it's a personal flaw or something to be proud of. There was actually a girl who used her MySpace account as a Sex in the ATX (Austin, TX like you didn't know), in which she would write devastating and witty write ups of her exploits.

I guess some of the former dates ran across the writings though and she had to make the account private.

Your resolve with your adorable smoking-like-a-chimney boy awes me - I run on a schedule about six times slower than you - definitely to my fault. I, frankly (and yes I'm being a big baby), do not think that the world is overfull of suitable Dara-boys. Which is why I like to try my best when I find one that does it for me. Though I appreciate your kind words. :-)

If you move to New York in this nebulous future, I will move with you. I am not horribly committed to my program. I like it, but ... I don't know about the five years. And then no choice of where I get to live - people seeking professor positions generally move where the job is, even if it be OHIO. Master's may be just fine for me. Is Massachusetts a gay mecca? I heard something to that effect the other day and wondered if that was why you drove across the country to it ... where else could Andy move? Hmmm. I jones for the big city and then small towns where I know everybody's name. What is Becca up to?

I'm off to eat Thai shrimp, of which there are four tupperwares of in my fridge, from last night's cooking. Pretty yummy let me tell you.

Bye!

Dara

From: Andrew Marx
To: dshifrer
Subject: RE: Better love next time, baby. - Dr. Hook
Date: Tue, 14 Nov 2006

Can you send me your current address? I can't recall where you moved to most recently (or when). You aren't still living in that house?

Re: boys
I would have hooked back up with my smoker-almost-bf in a heartbeat except he littered his e-mails with bizarre self-righteous platitudes and then started doing that thing where if something didn't work for him, he would try to hint at the issue rather than just say what he wanted to say. Would have been a lot more exciting if he had just wanted sex or something, but I never found out - if all he wanted was sympathy, boy did he date the wrong person. I refuse to speculate on the irony of having just accused him of self-righteous platitudes in light of having peppered e-mails to him with my own.

Online dating is not for me, I can't stand the inherent dishonesty. One guy tries to make it about meeting for coffee and then ends an e-mail with "So what do you like to do with guys?"

Interesting that you have me moving to New York. Any particular reason? I don't think Boston is an anything mecca. It's not a groovy, youthful place but people equate lots of small liberal arts colleges with liberal politics, sexual freedom and such open thought. The problem is that those very same small liberal arts colleges perpetuate exclusion and snobbery.

I've been in a righteous mood the last week or so. A friend of mine caught his wife cheating or maybe she admitted it outright, but in any case, the whole emotional trauma associated with going through it with him has just left me drained and feeling emotionally icky for him. Plus he's going to make it worse by clinging to some romantic notion of their marriage for years to come.

When did I become an adult with adult problems?

From: Dara Shifrer
To: amarx
Subject: if all he wanted was sympathy, boy did he date the wrong person
Date: Thu, 30 Nov 2006

Sorry about the address - it looks like you got it somehow. Thanks for the birthday card. Did I thank you already?

We had a cold front come in last night. EXCITING times for the Texans. We'd been a balmy 79 degrees for the entirety of the last two weeks and last night, the little leaves started stirring and temperatures were dropping 20 degrees within one hour. That's really it. It's in the thirties, everybody's wearing stocking caps indoors and there's some "moisture." Not sleet, snow or ice, though there is still hope being held out. My feet are really really cold. As I've gotten older, I've taken on my mother's annoying habit of being cold all of the time. I carry little sweaters around with me and even used to tie them around my waist until Michael accused me of becoming my mother.

Well, relieved to hear that there were flaws in the boy besides his depression/anxiety - no need to put up with self-righteous platitudes. Do you know who is ridiculously happy? Julianna! That Julianna! I've been moping about, crying a little every day - lots of problems with my sister and family as well - and I called Julianna and she was, as she said, "fucking a 26 year old." It kind of put me in my place. Who am I to be miserable when my reliably miserable friend isn't even miserable? She's lost 20 pounds and has switched from 50 year olds to 26 year olds as a result. There's a life secret for you.

New York ... because, where else is there? Do you long to go to St. Louis? Portland? I definitely don't see you in any of the Pacific Northwest cities. You've done the West Coast otherwise. We won't even consider the middle states for obvious reasons. I would tolerate Chicago. Actually, I think I'm moving Chicago up ahead of New York. Makes me feel warmer and fuller than New York.

Sorry to hear about the friend who was cheated on. Marriage is just appalling to me. We're actually on that right now for the Intro class that I TA for. She presents all of the data - 50% divorce, unequal divisions of labor, single women are happier (not the men though), etc. etc. and the silly kids still plan to do the same. She basically said that marriage was a social experiment of the 50s - not the norm before the 50s and ceasing to be the norm nowadays. Still, I find myself thinking sometimes about the 50% who don't divorce. Sociology is a big fat downer. Though not for people who don't subscribe to sympathy - you are just like Michael in that respect.

For some reason, my typing is having a delay time of 20 sec on the email today - it is annoying and I must return to Marx, Durkheim and Weber, my new best friends.

:-) Dara

From: Andrew Marx
To: dshifrer
Subject: RE: if all he wanted was sympathy, boy did he date the wrong person
Date: Thu, 30 Nov 2006

I talked to the boy today. Still attractive. He went to Europe for a month and I guess that renewed him a little. Not that I have ever done so, or could afford to even if I wanted to. I cannot even figure out how to get to Austin to visit. There is just no such thing in my budget as $350 for a plane ticket.

And as for the boy, I doubt I would get any further with him the second time around. I did think about asking but if I am going to date someone, I need to be treated well. I just think too many people are stuck in these relationships of spite and for what? It's disconcerting. Everyone fights and then stays in the relationship as though it's working. Shrug. That's why I'm single, I guess.

From: Dara Shifrer
To: amarx
Subject: Nah nah nah na nuh nah
Date: Mon, 8 January 2007

Guess who's coming to visit me!?! Your sister! Well, not me, but my city at least. I'm sure you already know. Why don't you join her for a couple days? You could stay at my house. I can't guarantee that I wouldn't be busy, but you'd have she and me to rely on for entertainment!

And how are you otherwise?

Dara

From: Andrew Marx
To: dshifrer
Subject: RE: Nah nah
Date: Tue, 9 Jan 2007

I did mention to my sister about coming down the last weekend Feb 9, 10 or something like that. I don't know, I don't always get a good vibe from my sister. I can't tell if I am intruding on her plans, or whatever. I know she wouldn't say no - after all, it's not like she's ever coming to Boston. But that's not the same thing, you know?

Anyway, I will probably NOT be coming to Austin in February. But if you promise to make some time for me, I will find a way to see you sometime this year. I will even let you pick the best time of the year for a visit. Or we can meet somewhere.

I'm back at work after a few weeks of lounging around, so it's alright. A tough transition to get up at 5:30 in the morning but I'll get my routine fired up in a couple of days. My website consumes most of my free time. No surprise.

From: Dara Shifrer
To: amarx
Subject: RE: Nah nah
Date: Tue, 9 January 2007

Lounging around! What have you been doing? Sick? New job? Holiday time off? Not to be nosy. Hopefully it was happy lounging around.

I understand the intruding thing - I hadn't thought of that. Actually, I am pretty certain that I will drive up the East coast this summer to visit all of you, but you, of course, are welcome to come to Austin some other time too.

Well I'm running late -

So late it's taken me 4 hours to send this email!!

Bye,

Dara

From: Andrew Marx
To: dshifrer
Subject: RE: Nah nah
Date: Tue, 9 Jan 2007

I spent the last two weeks on vacation. It was nice to work until 2 a.m. and then sleep all morning. This getting up at 6:00 a.m. is for the birds. It was a different routine. I like work, actually, moreso than I have in a while, but I can't help thinking how much more productive I would be in my real life if I had the extra 55 hours per week that I burn there.

From: Dara Shifrer
To: amarx
Subject: RE: Nah nah
Date: Sun, 14 January 2007

I totally understand the burn of burning so many hours at work that aren't your own. Has made me ill since I turned 22. Who knew our lives weren't going to be our own? You are particularly working long hours at 55/week. Glad you don't hate it right now. I am working with my advisor and really enjoying the work. Programming in SAS - a data analysis software. Have you used it? Or aware of it? So peaceful.

We're progressing toward a REALLY BIG storm. Probably nothing to you but Texas has her panties all bunched over it. I went to the grocery store last night - because that's what I do on Saturday nights now ;-) - and it was a big wreck because everybody felt the need to prepare for the REALLY BIG storm. Empty shelves ... gargantuan check-out lines. I guess I can't mock them though because there I was and here I am telling you about it. The weather men are falling all over themselves in delight.

I'm actually here at work, because that's what I do on Sundays now. Really it's just because I love this goddamn programming and haven't been able to stop thinking about how to correct my code, plus, I might be stuck at home tomorrow what with the REALLY BIG storm.

:-) Dara

From: Andrew Marx
To: dshifrer
Subject: RE: Nah nah
Date: Sun, 14 Jan 2007

No weather worries here this entire winter. Though single digit temperatures next week, they say. I guess. I need to hit the grocery store but lack the urgency. I have an extra day to shop because of the school holiday tomorrow. Maybe the weather will cooperate and I will feel like going out.

No news here, really. Just the Patriots win tonight against the San Diego Chargers and that's not really my news. You can get that on ESPN.

Hearing you talk about programming and fixing your code... man that's wild. What are you actually talking about?

Andy

From SmartReMarx.com
Ho! (Demo)
Posted by Andrew February 5, 2007

Check it out! My first song demo.

The song is called "Ho!" Now I just need to commission a remix.

It was really cold on the way home from work today (-3 wind chill factor) and this was the song I wrote in my head to distract myself from the creeping chill. Listen up! Am I ready for VH1 Storytellers or what?!?

"Ho! (Demo)" Lyrics

Bitches and Hos
Hos and Bitches
Bitches and Hos
Hos and Bitches
Hos and Bitches (bitches and hos)
Hos and Bitches (bitches and hos)

From: Andrew Marx
To: dshifrer
Subject: Sing-a-long
Date: Wed, 7 Feb 2007

Dara! Are you kidding? I haven't owned a car in two years. That's me WALKING from the bus stop in -3 degrees wind chill.

How was my sister's visit? Haven't heard from her since before she left.

From: Dara Shifrer
To: amarx
Subject: RE: Sing-a-long
Date: Sat, 10 Feb 2007

Walking, good god! Where's that old piece of shit car? Actually, after you said that, I do remember you making the big decision to go carless. That's insanity, but I guess you can take comfort late at night that YOU are not contributing to global warming like the rest of us sinners. That makes me laugh even harder than the thought of you rapping down the sidewalk.

Your sister is fantastic (must run in the family). But seriously, I saw her at Kerbey Lane earlier this week and was charmed anew - I meant to email you when I got home but my life is full of unfulfilled intentions lately ... She is just bright and happy and talks fast and has interesting things to say. Moreover, she seems very happy in her new life, which just makes it all the more fairytale. I just finished breakfasting with her and her college friends. She's returning to Britain in a couple of hours.

I am off to program like a mad woman.

:-) Dara

From: Andrew Marx
To: dshifrer
Subject: RE: Sing-a-long
Date: Mon, 12 Feb 2007

I made a pot of coffee this morning at work, and the other girl threw my pot out and made another one. I guess she didn't notice the coffeemaker was on and the pot was full?!? I think I'm going to make coffee tomorrow and see if it happens again.

I'm going to see Paula Cole this weekend. My first concert since June of last year. Seems longer. No, that's a lie, I saw Alice in Chains sometime last fall. This is Paula Cole's first concert in seven years, so I'm hoping. I have a shitty seat but I just decided it didn't matter.

I walk to work any day where the weather cooperates, basically no rain and over 10 degrees. It's worse when it's hotter. I can handle the cold but it's gross getting to work all sweaty on 70 degree mornings.

From: Dara Shifrer
To: amarx
Subject: Hppy Fckng Vlntn's Dy
Date: Wed, 14 Feb 2007

Sometimes I feel more kinship with you than any other human being. You are so refreshingly honest and frank, and don't hold back even if it displeases a person. Witty as hell. Smart as hell. And damn cute too. ;-)

From: Andrew Marx
To: dshifrer
Subject: RE: Hppy Fckng Vlntn's Dy
Date: Wed, 14 Feb 2007

Yeah, I like you better than most of my other friends, but if you repeat this to any of them, I'll say you forged the e-mail.

I'm finishing up my V-Day article. It's not about romance, let's just say that. We're having a major snow storm outside that is supposed to change to rain and freeze over. I'm pretty excited all around. I am also having a tough time with my reports this week and it's almost bringing me to the point of tears. Really hasn't been a productive week, but I'm trying to crank through them.

Lotsa love on this forlorn day!

AM

From: Dara Shifrer
To: amarx
Subject: RE: Hppy Fckng Vlntn's Dy
Date: Thu, 15 Feb 2007

"Your reports bring you to tears!" Wow, that school is doing a number on you. I refuse, outright refuse, to let any institution do that to me anymore! Well, I say that and then it happens but I'm always ashamed. I just lectured my youngest freakishly-over-achieving sister on this tonight - I told her that there's this old techno song that says "...And what do you say to the DJ!?! FUCK YOU!?!" and that it has forever inspired my inner dialogue when I am overwhelmed, pissed or anxious: "What do you say to the boy!?! FUCK YOU!" "What do you say to the boss!?! FUCK YOU!?!" It is conveniently universal and eternally relieving at the same time. And an ethic that I firmly believe in. Do as much for the soul-suckers as fits within your personal ethic, I told my sister. Man, she is a 22-year-old drama queen.

From: Andrew Marx
To: dshifrer
Subject: RE: Hppy Fckng Vlntn's Dy
Date: Fri, 16 Feb 2007

Maybe you should give the same talk to my youngest sibling. He's so shuttered. He doesn't think for himself, as far as I can tell, he doesn't want to. My parents are driving him towards a bachelor's program, but they don't seem to understand (or simply refuse to acknowledge) that he is only going to succeed at a four year program if he is driven to it himself. That's why I think it's a mistake to push him into it. It has to be important to him. All I can tell is that he wants everything to be handed to him so he doesn't have to make decisions or take responsibility for his actions. I was twenty-years old at one point too, so I totally get it. Transitioning to adulthood isn't all that exciting and in his case in particular because he thinks he's such a failure at everything.

I've talked to him extensively about it, but the bottom line is, I have no idea if he is listening. I told him that there are a myriad of options awaiting him, and that he just has to use his imagination a little. He's so fixated on a four year college but for no legitimate reason. He wants to please his parents, and rightly so (they pay the bills) so I do get that. But a trade school would make a lot more sense, or something more directed towards his interests so that he can build some credibility within himself. I mean, if they're paying tuition anyway, maybe he should be more practical about it - an acting school or art school. And I told him specifically that if he made a reasonable presentation of a full-time activity that wasn't necessarily a four year college, that his parents would support him.

I'm not giving up on him, I don't think anyone has. But at some point, he has to be entrusted to figure it out for himself.

This week at work ended more productively, less humiliation.

From Concert-Central.com
Paula Cole, Berklee Performance Theatre, Boston, MA February 16, 2007
Review by Andrew

Cole arranged for a hometown performance at the Berklee Performance Theatre, a part of the Berklee College of Music where Cole attended. She was greeted warmly by a mix of friends, fans and college students. Her first tune was an amazing reworking of one of her biggest hits Where Have All The Cowboys Gone? Cole sat alone on stage, at the piano and played a new arrangement of the song. It was breathtaking. She followed by adding drummer Ben Wittman for a roaring version of Mississippi from her album This Fire.

Most of the set stole from This Fire, the one album that made Paula Cole a household name, however briefly - though it is not besides the point that she won a Grammy for Best New Artist in 1998. During the two hour set, she addressed the audience openly and often, talking about her experiences in the seven years she was away from the music scene, about her new energy and her musical influences.

Cole's voice is better than it has ever sounded, and it was always an impressive instrument in its own right. She looked radiant and happy and the performance was as nice a treat for the audience as it was for her.

From: Andrew Marx
To: dshifrer
Subject: Ham Day
Date: Tue, 20 Feb 2007

Well, Dara. I slept a lot of the weekend instead of working on the concert-central site. Part of me says, if I'm sleeping that much, I probably needed it. I actually was very productive in my waking hours of the weekend.

Paula Cole only got reviewed by the Globe, so not much in the way of competition for my review. Plus, I included the setlist for her show, and people are always looking for that. She was pretty awesome. I think the band will be better once they have played on the road together. The set was great but there was some stoppage and momentum didn't build as much as it might after they've been playing together longer.

Someone made cinnamon pumpkin muffins this morning to DIE for.

And the best part, someone is giving me a ham tomorrow. A full HAM! I get to take it home and cook it over the weekend. I'm stoked.

From: Andrew Marx
To: dshifrer
Subject: "Before it's news, it's buzz" Andy Marx
Date: Tue, 20 Mar 2007

Oh Dara! I went to a St. Patrick's Day gathering at my friend Jeremy's house. He made (ack!) key lime pie, green whip cream and mint green cake. Oh my God they were gross, but I only told him that key lime wasn't my thing and just sort of left off about the mint frosting. He's a really good chef usually. And I hate Irish creme, so end of the evening coffee really wasn't much of a reward for me.

Andy

From: Dara Shifrer
To: amarx
Subject: RE: "Before it's news, it's buzz" Andy Marx
Date: Wed, 21 Mar 2007

Damn thing just deleted my email to you.

So anyway, one more time.

The concert site was in my thoughts all week last week as I took notes on many many South by Southwest shows. I didn't get a wristband for SXSW, and so am casting the week's experience as more deficient than I probably ought to be. A lot of the bands that are in town for SXSW perform free shows, and so we tried to hit several but it's still a bit of a clusterfuck even so. I actually saw bands from all over the place (even outside of the US), and need to stop acting like a spoiled Austinite - all of these distorted expectations for live music. Anyway, my point is that I'm looking forward to posting the reviews on the concert site!!!

I didn't do anything for St Patrick's Day but squirm at the people walking around with shamrock stickers down their sleeves and on their hats and such. All bleery eyed drunk. But, of course, being in Boston, I suppose it's quite the deal. I don't know Jeremy, but it was exciting to hear you mention names - your social life has been very cloudy of late. Chef friends are great friends to have. Unless, of course, they don't respect your food preferences.

I went to a funeral for my mom's brother two weekends ago, and then tried to accomplish everything I hadn't had time for (work for my advisor) as well as attend several shows a night, and so am hugely relieved that spring break is over. They defamed my uncle at the funeral! Not sure if that is typical, but I enjoyed it hugely. Funerals really are a spectacle - human drama and such.

Well, my time to work has come.

Bye bye!

From Concert-Central.com
Girl Fart, being pulled by a truck down Red River, Austin, TX
March 15, 2007
Review by Dara

Mostly exciting because set up on a piece of cardboard being pulled by a truck - inventive way to participate in SXSW? Seemed a good band as well - young, psychedelic. Experimental says Rockboy.

From Concert-Central.com
Todd and the Rank Outsiders, Hole in the Wall, Austin, Texas
March 17, 2007
Review by Dara

They're from Los Angeles - in town for South by Southwest. Like Bob Seger on speed or, as Rockboy says, a punk Van Morrison. The lead singer has a very distinct persona - dances in native-man circles howling like a wolf in his feather earring. Just a mystic cheese rocker in the end - terrible but loveable. Seemed close to the young punk in the band. They sang one great blues song that was taught to him by an old Louisiana man named Percy.

WHITTLED AWAY EMOTIONALLY TO THE CORE

---- Original Message ----
From: Dara Shifrer
To: amarx
Subject: RE: Concert Site
Date: Mon, 9 Apr 2007

Okay, this is too much fun - and can you please add 'prog rock' to the category list?

From: Dara Shifrer
To: amarx
Subject: RE: Concert Site
Date: Mon, 9 Apr 2007

Sorry to be a pain, but can you add surf, psychedelia, and rockabilly.

Chapter Seven *Whittled Away Emotionally To The Core*

From Concert-Central.com
Chop Tops, Red 7, Austin, TX July 13, 2007
Review by Dara

Rockabilly outfit from Santa Cruz, good but so much the same I think the time has come for me and this genre to part ways, did have one good surf guitar song, singer verged between social critique and ignorant obnoxiousness, spit at small crowd and tossed his drumstick at Rockboy but all in good fun you know, covered Stray Cats, highlight of the show was a fight between a girl in a polka-dotted dress and a girl with pink hair that matched her pink frothy dress

My disdain for genre/band is less an accurate perception and more a result of personal events that evening, Chop Tops is a good band

---- Original Message ----
From: Andrew Marx
To: dshifrer
Subject: I Got a Life
Date: Sun, 12 Aug 2007

Hey Daralicious,

Well, business first: I wanted you to know that the concert site is now indexed, which means people are finding it through natural searches and my dear, your stuff is getting read.

That may excite me way more than you, but I thought you should know.

Anyway, I had wanted to start going to some shows on a more regular basis but I just keep pushing it back as a priority. But thank you for your hard work.

Things here are peachy. Last week sucked, but it was just related to my energy level, nothing more or less specific than that. Football has started again this week, so that puts on me on Cloud 9 until the Super Bowl (January, give or take). Plus the Patriots are way favored this year.

I heard from Becca but all she wanted to talk about was you and Julianna, which I thought was weird and evasive. Like, it wasn't uncomfortable at all, it was just that was 20 minutes of conversation about Julianna's move. (Which is so insignificant to me). I guess that means we don't have anything else to talk about? Feh. The Vegas thing seems pretty far away now. It's been a whole year since I was there. And this will be the first year I don't go back, I think. I missed the summer season and the winter doesn't look so promising for travel.

My friend convinced me to sign up for match.com - but so far it's not going. Well, I e-mail guys but they don't e-mail back and I haven't been contacted directly by anyone. I don't know, I feel like if you're going to pay for a service, you should be more open to at least e-mailing back, or even just meeting someone once - even if they aren't the ideal. But someone else told me summer's never a good time to use online dating. I will dutifully to try to stay a member for longer than the refundable 3 day-window.

Alright, Sunday Night Football.

Andyatomy

From: Dara Shifrer
To: amarx
Subject: RE: I Got a Life
Date: Tue, 14 Aug 2007

Hey Andy-drop,

Really!?! That is exciting and worrisome - I kind of thought nobody would ever see the concert site. I worry that I might hurt the feelings of one of the artists or reveal something about my social life that I shouldn't. And I have still been posting! I did stop while I was in Belize b/c of lack of access. Some of the shows are free but most charge a cover at the door, from $3 to $15. There are bigger venues here that have shows that require Ticketmaster or whatever, but I tend to avoid those because they're so much more expensive and because there are so many viable alternatives. This is why I love Austin. Boston has a scene too though, or so I seem to hear.

It is so funny to me that you're such a football nut. I've probably told you but I have a thing for it as background noise. It reminds me of homes and autumn and boys I've liked. But insofar as watching it... I don't think so...

Well, speaking of, Becca just recently got into touch with Julianna and I both - basically copied one e-mail into the other. All that she talked about was you.

It is very interesting to me that summer is not an ideal time for online dating - I can't imagine why. Julianna has had tremendous success with it here - to my mind at least. The girl has been single and/or dating men twice her age for the last five years, and within a month of signing up with the FREE Plenty of Fish, she went on 4-5 dates and had some follow-up as well. She canceled her account because none of them were The One and she'd 'had enough,' but I thought that was a might bit unreasonable. I have visions of going on horrid dates and writing funny little write ups about them but I suppose it would wear on me.

Hope you're having another peachy week,

Dara

From: Andrew Marx
To: dshifrer
Subject: RE: I Got a Life
Date: Tue, 14 Aug 2007

I might go to a show next week; I have a running list of concerts that I want to go to. It's like that, not that I'm planning to go but I am always "in consideration."

I am failing miserably at online dating. No one has contacted me and barely responded to my e-mails (I send out a few a week just to try and wring every cent out of my membership). Even my friend who recommended match.com (which by the way is expensive) is surprised by the total lack of response. He keeps saying so as if that's supposed to make me feel better.

Well, whatever. I will just keep trying until my membership expires. I just don't figure out how everyone else isn't as desperate as I am.

AM

From Concert-Central.com
Bangladesh, Emo's, Austin, TX August 18, 2007
Review by Dara

This was the indoors show and what a difference it was: death-metal / screamo with some rap nuances and I couldn't stop giggling at them, they took themselves way too seriously, so full of their own testosterone had to take the shirts off, eyes rolling back in the head, Jesus poses, and all the 18 year olds in the crowd throwing devil horns, very very intense and I suppose they're good at what they do, dreadlocked 45 year old (possibly 25 and just wracked by drugs) suddenly turned to me and pointed to his eye... his heart... and then me... I stood out in my skirt and heels, the merchandise metalhead gave me a stack of stuff for free because I asked the name of the band.

From: Dara Shifrer
To: amarx
Subject: Jesus Loves You But Everybody Else Thinks You're an Asshole
Date: Mon, 20 Aug 2007

Your running list of shows in consideration is likely a much more serious affair than the piddle I see - music is just intertwined into the social scene in Austin though I do make an effort to partake. You go to the real thing. You should send me your intended list - I would be interested in that - I know my intended list is much more interesting than what I actually end up seeing. I just looked at November 2005 and was astounded at how often I was seeing music that month - makes me wonder what exactly causes a flurry like that. I keep track of who I went to the shows with in my personal file and so it's always an exercise of nostalgia to post them.

Speaking of, kind of, I was googling something the other day and this little vignette turned up and so I started reading it and enjoying it which turned out to be because it was my own story!! And then I was very upset because it had extremely personal information about a friend in it and was never posted online. And then I was relieved when I figured out that Google has a new function called Google Desktop that includes your desktop in every internet search. But then I was confused when I realized that that particular document may have been stored on my laptop at some point but had long ago been deleted... My question is: does the computer never delete anything but actually store it forever for future inconvenient pop-ups? It just bothers me to have so little control over where my documents are going. I've been backing up my flash drive on my personal drive at work (because there's so much space) but now I'm worried about the personal stuff that is also on my flash drive. Advice, please, computer guru.

Well, I do think there's a whole science to online dating profiles. A science I don't understand but there are resources/sources out there. How to dupe the other person into falling for you with the right mask. I ran across some propaganda from a Christian Carter, a man who teaches women how to overcome their man's non-committal distant stance. He reduces it to five main points, and all within the woman's control. The straightforward approach to the love mystery appeals to me. The weight of responsibility on the woman enrages me. I am totally engrossed by this man. I have been forwarding the unsolicited emails I receive from him to Julianna and Morgan (my littlest sister), and even my two most tolerant audiences have been chiding me. The man speaks to me. Don't laugh but his tagline is: catch him and keep him. I've clearly hit a low point in my life. My point is, if you want to mastermind potential lovers, you can do it! I would guess a lot of the guys on Match.com are intimidated by your intelligence. And everybody is desperate and it seems like problems could mutually be solved if people would get on top of the matter, literally, but I guess people aren't as desperate as they think?

From: Andrew Marx
To: dshifrer
Subject: RE: Jesus Loves You
Date: Mon, 20 Aug 2007

My sister is coming to visit. And apparently SO are my parents. They are driving up from New York. The whole thing is a little vague to me but there's dinner involved, of course.

I had brunch with Becca. She wanted an awful lot to talk about you and Julianna - I didn't have much to contribute. But we had a good time. Surprisingly, I guess.

From: Dara Shifrer
To: amarx
Subject: RE: Jesus Loves You
Date: Tue, 21 Aug 2007

Hmm, this obsession with Julianna and me is odd. I don't understand it. She makes very little effort to stay in touch with me, which doesn't upset me, but surprises me that I/we are so much in her range of thoughts. Maybe she was nervous and just making conversation. Julianna has this idea that she is constantly talking shit about her and/or me which is probably true. Not that Julianna and I refrain all that much. Glad that it went well though!

I just can't figure out how they even find the site. I tried googling white rabbits last night and didn't see your site in the first few pages... Is there something we could put in each headline that would attract more hits? Like concert or show or band or some other common word? How do you think they come across the site?

From: Andrew Marx
To: dshifrer
Subject: At Least I Know What I'm Missing
Date: Tue, 21 Aug 2007

Google blogsearch is more likely to show results of the reviews by artist, but it also favors newer posts so that they come up first. That might explain why the White Rabbits review did not hit in the first few pages of results.

Speaking of Becca, you know I just don't know. Julianna is such an out of sight, out of mind kind of person, which does not endear me to her much. But it's always interesting to see if she picked up different gossip than I did.

From: Dara Shifrer
To: amarx
Subject: And You Smell Like a Monkey Too
Date: Thu, 30 Aug 2007

Happy birthday to you.
Happy birthday to you.
HappPPPPY BIRRRRTHDAAAYYY DEAARR ANNNN -
DEEEE!
Happy birthday to you.

From: Andrew Marx
To: dshifrer
Subject: RE: And You Smell Like a Monkey Too
Date: Thu, 30 Aug 2007

Even if I smell like a monkey, I look hot today. Thanks!

From: Dara Shifrer
To: amarx
Subject: See Your True Colors
Date: Sat, 8 Sep 2007

I love love your Debbie Harry and Cyndi Lauper posts. And I
cannot believe that you remember what you saw in 1988. Yes
I just looked that far down the list. Do you write things down
(like 1988 concerts and current set lists) or are you just that
good?

From: Andrew Marx
To: dshifrer
Subject: RE: See Your True Colors
Date: Sat, 8 Sep 2007

I have been taking notes on the concerts since about 1997, so
it was then that I backtracked when 1988 was only 10 years
ago and not twenty. AC/DC was my first concert ever. I forget
how young I was. It was a rough-and-tumble audience full of
leather and tats and ring girls. I was scared as shit the entire
time.

I really like Debbie Harry's music but I can't figure out the appeal of her live show. It was like hearing it over the PA in a wax museum. I'm going to see Mixfest this year with Matchbox Twenty and Daughtry. So that ought to be interesting, as I am decidedly not an American Idol devotee. Tickets were expensive, $70 something. So you probably get the better end of the deal by seeing the cheap/free shows.

My parents are in town next week. First it was 90 degrees, now they are calling for rain. Does the weather lady not understand how this works? Neither of those weather forecasts is acceptable. I invited my parents to work and will give them a tour - if they are willing to get out of the car. Unfortunately for them, you can't really see anything from the road.

Megan and husband will be here next weekend, so that ought to be a change of pace.

From Concert-Central.com
True Colors Tour, Bank of America Pavilion, Boston, MA June 16, 2007
Review by Andrew

Cyndi Lauper is otherworldly. There is no other way to describe her performance. To the opening chords of Hole in My Heart, she stood behind a white ceiling-to-floor curtain, visible only by her silhouette before she came out on stage adorned in a wide umbrella hat decorated in rainbow color stripes and a long black wig. She wore an inexplicable outfit that looked like a flak jacket dress with S&M straps that seemed neither functional nor decorative. She tore across the stage through every song, as if trying to reach out to every single person in the audience. She never lacked for energy, never suffered a dull moment even with technical difficulties marring her entire set. During one pause between songs, Cyndi explained that the doctor shut her mother's legs right as she was cresting, to make her grand entrance into the world, "and I ain't been the same every since!" she screamed before ripping off her wig to reveal the shock of short, purple hair underneath.

Erasure's 45 minute set came near the tail end of the night, just as the sun had set. Though the five hour equality lovefest was never dull, the timing of Erasure's disco-tinged, non-stop rotation of familiar dance hits was a welcome boost of energy. Backed by three singers, Andy Bell and Vince Clarke came out on stage in matching vintage Blondie t-shirts with the words "Platinum Blonde" on the front in silver glitter. Vince wore army fatigues over his shirt and a platinum blonde wig. Andy looked good, just as seriously sexy at 43 years old as he was in 1985.

Debbie Harry moved like a glacier across the stage, bouncing in place like a bobble head for long periods of time and then drifting to other points on the stage. Her crystalline voice was untarnished by a thirty plus year career and the music overall was enjoyable, but there was something so wooden and awkward about her stage presence, it riveted all your attention. During guitar solos, she moved to the back of the stage to stand placidly in the shadow of the drum set to await her turn. The closest she got to animated was a little Tina Turner kick but mostly, it was like watching the wax figurine of Debbie Harry sing Debbie Harry songs.

The Dresden Dolls are the kind of band that cannot be described by mere words, but I'll try anyway. One half Amanda Palmer and one half Brian Viglione, they are self-described as punk cabaret. It's a fitting, however limited, description. They came on stage calmly. Amanda was outfitted in fishnet stockings and a corset and Brian in a white nightgown, with his face painted mime white, pajama-bottoms with his underwear on the outside. This was a hits show of sorts. They knew that the audience would be largely unfamiliar and pulled out some of their best known songs including Shores of California and Coin-Operated Boy. Amanda does the singing, pounding on her keyboards while Brian accompanies on drums, and once, guitar.

Margaret Cho started her night as hostess of the True Colors Tour subdued by saying frankly, "We're all happy Jerry Falwell is dead." Yes, that was subdued. Cho was happily inserted between each band while the crew changed sets behind her with marvelous efficiency, giving us small chunks of her stand-up routine that got dirtier as the night went on.

From: Andrew Marx
To: dshifrer
Subject: Too ease for the man
Date: Tue, 18 Sep 2007

Dara, did you see Supersuckers twice in the same night in May, or is that a typo?

I realize one was a promo-appearance at Waterloo's so I thought maybe it was right, but then the description of the two performances is so different, I couldn't tell. So I thought I would ask.

I'm having a bad week. Post-family recovery. Parents visited at the beginning of last week, and sister and husband came to Boston at the end. I'm exhausted and whittled away emotionally to the core. Yeah, life does seem to spiral out of control. On the other hand, I kind of like it that way. I have to force myself to slow down and take a deep breath once in a while. And because everything seems so accelerated, I tend to go go go and then face a weekend of total collapse.

Mostly all we did was a series of family dinners last week. Still had to work during the day when they were here. Whenever I spend time with my father and step-mother, they always ask me if I'm dating. They have this new thing where they try to brainstorm men that I can be with (usually not men in my age bracket because of course, they don't actually know anyone younger than 40) and then take pictures of me from different angles, like getting a panoramic x-ray of your jaw at the dentist. Usually while I'm eating so there's a fork in my hand and some food dribbling out of my mouth. Can't wait to see the personal ad that comes out of those.

I'm irritable and irascible and other ir-words but I don't know if that's any more frequently than at other times. I like my family a lot these days, but a lot more from a distance.

I didn't feel relaxed even with my sister here, I don't know what it was. Anyway, I have a week to recover then I am hosting Marie for a weekend. That should be fun. We're going to see

Mixfest, and I think we have dinner plans Friday night with Josephine and her financee. (?? Two ee's for the guy??)

Speaking of Josephine, we went out for dinner around my birthday. She, who is a vegan-adjacent and doesn't eat cheese, mentioned her allergies to our waitress and every two minutes, someone in management would come over to our table to take her pulse and make sure they hadn't killed her. It wasn't entirely unjustified. After ordering pasta hold-the-cheese, the food expediter brought her pasta with cheese. So she says to the waitress, "Well I won't *die* if I eat it" exactly like you would say it if, in fact, you would die.

Feh. E-mail over.

From: Dara Shifrer
To: amarx
Subject: Whittled Away Emotionally to the Core
Date: Wed, 19 Sep 2007

Amazing! Very exciting!

The Supersuckers did play twice - a promo just as you said - the differences speak to the fact that my reviews are largely a function of my mood, daily events, etc. I realized as I was posting those that they had been written linearly and wouldn't be that way on the site but I was in a hurry frankly. I also feel some compulsion to retain the purity of my original writing, which is silly. I think the Waterloo was an acoustic set as well - I'll have to check with Michael. Would make a big difference.

So great that you brought up family and the woes therein involved... I am heading to visit mine tomorrow and it has been the cloud on my life for the last week. I'm actually kind of looking forward to it at this point - b/c as you say I like them a lot - but they wrack me! They make me angrier and sadder than most people have the power to...Purportedly, everything is kosher over there at this time but still... Megan didn't delight you? She seems to get to America quite a bit. I don't hear from her anymore. I guess the occasional mass email but more occasional than otherwise lately. Tell me her gossip if you remember.

I have no idea how you spell male future-spouses.

All right, I am off to pack, find a ride and find a Crahobi caretaker!

Dara

From: Andrew Marx
To: dshifrer
Subject: RE: Whittled Away Emotionally to the Core
Date: Wed, 3 Oct 2007

How old is your cat? I feel like it's been alive for ages (unless you've been secretly replacing it with a new Crahobi every year like switching out air fresheners???)

So. Josephine's fiancé, Jack, is trying to twist my arm to go with them on a December Vegas trip. I'm ambivalent about the trip. Or maybe indecisive. I could look up some friends from college if I was going to be there anyway. But it's not a reason by itself to go.

I have to diverge to tell you how smart my spell checker is, Dara. I was spelling fiancée with two ee's and it somehow divined that Josephine was a woman's name and the appropriate spelling of fiancé in the possessive that came directly after her name was of the male variety. I have no idea how lesbian couples are going to be able negotiate the spell-checker. Very carefully, one thinks.

From: Dara Shifrer
To: amarx
Subject: RE: Whittled Away Emotionally to the Core
Date: Mon, 8 Oct 2007

I know! Sometimes I look at my cat and I can't believe he's stuck by me as long as he has. As a matter of fact, I have been with him longer than I have any man. Pretty sad statement on the state of Dara's life. He's a good egg. I was out for lunch with a girl friend and was very disappointed when she felt it necessary to tell me the long long story of the death of her dog, but by the end I was a little teary eyed and determined to go home and give Crahobi the attention he deserves. The breaking point was when she described pulling out of her driveway and seeing the silhouette of her dog on the porch and then remembering that he was no longer able to silhouette.

Vegas again! Sounded like a pretty agonizing decision for you but at least it will be with a different crowd than last time. You have a lot more connection to Vegas than I do it seems - in terms of the city at least. Got to be the gambling.

I don't know what to do for Thanksgiving. I have actually been invited to Las Vegas but it would involve more drinking than I am interested in frankly. I could of course go home but there's always Christmas to be stressed out about. Is your sister coming back to the states for Thanksgiving too?

It is October 9th and as hot as my pancake griddle today. I am not pleased.

From: Andrew Marx
To: dshifrer
Subject: RE: Whittled Away Emotionally to the Core
Date: Mon, 8 Oct 2007

I don't feel stellar today, but I have dutifully come into work for the sole purpose, apparently, of reading e-mails until 5pm. There's no a/c in the office today. I guess it's the annual switch to winter heating in our building. I've been here 10 minutes and I want to die it's so warm. It's been rough seas lately. I'm not sure what the cure is. Probably less nights carousing.

My friend Josephine's fiancé Jack has adopted me as some kind of orphan. He always checks in to see how I'm doing and gets me invited places I have no business being. I'm sure he does this with other friends, but I'm highly pleased to be on the VIP list.

I'm basically torn about everything these days. Vegas is just on the list somewhere of things to decide, between tattoos (violates the principles of Judaism - not that religion has ever been a guiding principle in adulthood) and Halloween costuming (pagan rituals masquerading as secular tradition - and don't get me started on the fact that as a country, America does not need any more candy). I don't where decisive-Andy went to, but he's not answering his pages. Can you believe I just referred to myself as an adult? The self-delusions are just whittling away.

In other news, I told my mom I still hadn't bought tickets to Oakland to visit her yet and her response was

ok

That's it. Just

ok

No caps, full sentence or anything. Where's the motherly concern? Sheesh.

AM

From: Dara Shifrer
To: amarx
Subject: It's only a sad dog that doesn't wag its own tail
Date: Fri, 26 Oct 2007

I noticed the date on your unreplied-to-email the other day and was appalled at how much time had passed. It immediately brought to mind the swift passing of life and the imminence of death. I'm not kidding. The days and weeks are like dripping syrup since October started. And I'm turning 31 in a couple of weeks - like 30 wasn't already appallingly old.

"Decisive Andy"!! Were you making a big funny? Do you really perceive yourself as decisive? I would say you're more of the agonizing type... but what do I know? Maybe you agonize with decisiveness. It brings to mind that Harry and Sally line: you're the worst kind, you're high maintenance and think you're low-maintenance... something like that. Lines from that movie always come to me.

Glad to hear you've been adopted and are carousing at night. I had to put a sharp stop to my carousing. I stay home now and with a vengeance. The greatest satisfaction that I get from life is working on my programming with music in my headphones - bliss. I'm sure that bad Dara will resurface at some point. Julianna's a bad influence I'm telling you. Our roles have been reversed. We're actually supposed to go kayaking in the moonlight tonight. It's only $5 and sounds like ridiculous fun to me. But what a hassle! We're all also given glowstick necklaces to wear which is just silly.

It hit me that your family might be affected by the fires in California. Are they okay? The smoke has even drifted to Apple Valley - my mom sent an email saying they had shut down the schools because of low air quality. But I know San Diego is among the hardest hit.

Dara

From: Andrew Marx
To: dshifrer
Subject: RE: It's only a sad dog
Date: Sat, 27 Oct 2007

A lot of people I know were in the general path of the raging fires in San Diego. Though in Boston, there was not a peep about anything going on in the news until Tuesday night. I got an e-mail from my friend whose parents live in Leucadia. That was the first I heard of anything. It still wasn't covered very much on CNN or the less legitimate news sources. Nancy Grace is all about Britney Spears these days. There was some question about how Britney was managing back and forth between her burning homes in LA and Malibu.

(I was going to make a joke about second-hand smoke, too, but maybe it's not funny-time).

I heard from my dad and family a few times, but none of their homes were in the direct path of a fire. I assume that hasn't changed since Tuesday since nobody e-mailed after that.

From Concert-Central.com
Cracker, Mohawk, Austin, TX November 2, 2007
Review by Dara

One of my favorite shows ever, I loved this band and love them still, eerie to see the man with the voice I've heard for so many years, incredible variety in their music from slow country dearths to jumpy punk to plain old rock to quirky indie, but always dark, one of the cleanest most professional sounding bands I've ever seen, I want so badly to sit with him on a porch on the California beach, he's a wise man, oh and he was wearing a white hoody with rainbow-colored lines across it because he's cool like that and doesn't care

CHRISTMAS TIME AGAIN

---- Original Message ----
From: Andrew Marx
To: dshifrer
Subject: RE:
Date: Sun, 15 Apr 2007

I had a fun "boys night" last night at a new casino in Rhode Island. It was super trashy and it totally wiped me out today.

From: Dara Shifrer
To: amarx
Subject: RE:
Date: Tue, 17 Apr 2007

A super trashy boys night at a casino - sounds pretty exciting. I think I was finding percentages of girls who played softball in the 70s versus the 80s versus the 90s ...

From SmartRemarx.com
New Casino Smell at Twin River April 16, 2007
Posted by Andrew

Just days before we were heading down to Lincoln, Rhode Island for a night of slot machine fun at Twin River, I saw my first commercial for the newly renovated gambling hall. The ad spot featured a cascade of multi-ethnic middle-aged people dancing to the refrain "Take Me to the River" while blurry images of slot machines and plates of food rushed by in the background.

The commercial's producers opted to dub the song from an old, deeply-grooved Al Green vinyl that plays that one line from the song in a continuous, tuneless loop. Maybe they didn't get permission to use the song, or maybe they are just all tone deaf. Whatever the thinking behind the commercial, it comes off painfully amateur. (You can hear the "song" on the property's website).

Twin River is the completely renovated gaming property at Lincoln Park. The new owners admitted the need to overhaul the entire property from top to bottom from electrical wiring to the glittering gaming floor to food operations. What it became is a decidedly Rhode Island ghetto version of its Connecticut brethren, Foxwoods and Mohegan Sun. Everything about Twin River is a second generation photocopy of the Connecticut casinos, themselves already copies of Vegas-style mega-resorts.

Driving up to the property, it's not entirely clear by any signage or even the spectacle of the building that you have arrived. It looks like a warehouse or an airport remote parking lot. Walking through the main entrance is the closest to a Vegas-feel that you get anywhere on the property. You have the canopied valet lanes and then the wide expanse of glass doors leading into the casino and you get a sense of mimicry of what a modern casino tends to be.

The bulk of the casino is what you see immediately on the main floor. Twin River is only slot machines and state scratcher tickets, no table games, no keno balls and no poker tables. It is just rows and rows of modern slot machines that take money in and spit tickets back out. Like most casinos, Twin River doesn't deal in coin anymore, it's purely a paper in-paper out system of gambling.

For those who aren't old enough to remember when coin was the currency of slot machines, those were glorious days when your hands turned black and your fingers smelled like metal and you would scoop up all your winnings into a cup and, if you won big, it was a real triumph carrying around eight pounds of quarters. These days you slip the redemption ticket into your jacket pocket and carry it around with you until you're ready to leave.

It's easy to be underwhelmed by Twin River. Despite the profusion of slots, they mostly seem the same after a while. Okay maybe that's true at any casino, but the website specifically touts this distinction: "you're always one step away from the 3rd largest variety of video slot machines in the nation." There's something so weird about being so proud of that. That's so...Rhode Island. Woohoo!

We're third! Take that Taj Mahal!

Twin River's distinguishing features included androgynous restrooms, clouds of cigarette smoke, and MILF soccer mom cocktail waitresses. On the casino floor, high above the bank of slots were flat screens displaying sexy hot Paris Hilton videos (oh you read that right, she has more than one - I have seen the proof). The second floor was restaurant row and another smaller room of slot machines. The restaurant choices were the generic steakhouse, the generic Irish pub, the generic food court, the generic family restaurant and the generic buffet. The food at the generic buffet was actually pretty good. Thumbs up the beef, thumbs down the pasta. Thumbs up the mashed potatoes and pizza, thumbs down, way down, for anything on the dessert tray that wasn't the ice cream.

We wandered the first floor for a few hours, ate at the buffet and wandered the second floor for a few hours. After a while, it became evident that 200,000 square feet wasn't as big as it sounds. Maybe I was wrong for comparing it to Mohegan Sun, or even Las Vegas itself. But in the end, Twin River was pretty much just a third-rate gambling experience.

But I'm guessing for the locals, that's just like first place!

8

Chapter Eight *Christmas Time Again*

---- Original Message ----
From: Andrew Marx
To: dshifrer
Subject: Our Lips Are Sealed
Date: Fri, 16 Nov 2007

I'm leaving for CA this weekend and hopefully a few days of leisure. I have to organize my iPod for travel with my A-list of songs and eat all the eggs in my fridge.

Oh, and I guess pack. I don't plan on taking much. I'll think about laundry tomorrow but laundry is one of those things I almost want to pay someone else to do for me. It is taxing and just not very rewarding use of my time except on really cold winter days when you take a freshly laundered shirt out of the dryer and put it on. That's the life.

Becca called me this week, but when I called her back, she didn't answer. I'm guessing she's about the same.

I'm rather looking forward to the trip, but I hope that enthusiasm remains once I'm there. I often feel like it's a really long trip, and there won't be any siblings around so it's really just me and dinners with my mother. I don't know who is coming for Thanksgiving dinner. I might have to make small talk the entire meal!

AM

From: Dara Shifrer
To: amarx
Subject: RE: Our Lips Are Sealed
Date: Sat, 17 Nov 2007

I enjoyed your little to-do list of an email. Your Thanksgiving sounds a little painful except for the prepared iPod. Do you know that I still don't own an MP3 player? If I buy one, they'll come out with the next new product the following week so you'd better hope that I restrain myself.

Why aren't your siblings going home for Thanksgiving? I can guess why Megan isn't but the others? My whole family is going to Las Vegas to visit my youngest sister who lives there now. I should go but eh... they are exhausting. And I saw them recently. And I'll see them in nearly a month. Everybody here is whining about the price of plane tickets for Christmas time: $500 no matter where they're flying. I don't know if it's a national epidemic or if it's just Austin.

I am in collapse mode. I haven't seriously worked since Wednesday. I tried so hard today and kept returning to the couch or the bed.

Fortunately I saw two very good movies: Puccini for Beginners and Sleeping Dogs Lie. I dreamt during a nap on Thursday that I couldn't breathe and I couldn't tell the people sitting on the couch near me and I could feel myself panicking, thinking I was going to die, and I kept trying to tell myself it was just an anxiety attack - though I've never had one in real life before. It was an unusual dream for me. I also have a mole on my neck that is itchy and scabbed over - has been for over a week now - so I am certain that I am in the early stages of melanoma. So, my point is, I have decided that I am seriously but understatedly depressed.

I think Julianna is co-opting all of my friends here. She's just a better friend than I. Always looking to hang out, always calling, you know her. What are you going to do? Conversely, I have been feeling overwhelmed by the social demands being placed on me and trying to avoid people because all that I really want to do is stay home.

It's finally fall here. Fat brown leaves and some rain today. I do love that.

From: Andrew Marx
To: dshifrer
Subject: Four Beers and I'm Andy
Date: Tue, 20 Nov 2007

I'm trying to charge my iPod but it wasn't happy to be plugged into my mother's computer while I was working on anything else, so I'm going to have to charge it while I'm watching a movie in another room.

Megan doesn't always attend TG at my mom's house since her move to England. My brother and wife are entertaining her parents in New York City for TG. I don't know if she's cooking or if they are going out for festive dinner. My youngest brother is in Nebraska, doing God knows what, I think he works at a car wash or some such nonsense. He thinks he's going back to college in another year, but I think that's all just a front to keep the parents from going completely berserk. I think of all the sibs, he's still in that place where he's running as far from family as he can get (not that Nebraska would have been my first choice, but maybe it's unexpectedly serene to find yourself lost in a corn field).

Did you do anything last weekend for your birthday (or I guess it didn't have to be over the weekend…)

New Year's has me in a tear. I've been invited to a party by my friend Jack. It's going to be a lot of people I've never met and a lot of drinking and God knows what else and I just don't do well in crowds at all (though four beers and I'm friendly).

Such dilemmas. Last year, I was Marie's in Burlington, but that party was very sedate even though there was drinking and everyone was super nice. It was an ice sheet around midnight so the drive home which was still less than a mile was fraught with excitement.

Have a wonderful one.

From *SmartReMarx.com*
Who the Hell Wants to Live in California? November 23, 2007
Posted by Andrew

I love people from New England. They have no problem being trapped in a house surrounded on all sides by twenty-four feet of snow (which for the record, is four times my height and cold) but a tiny tremor in the earth caused by two tectonic plates playing chicken, and the world is coming to an end. Don't get me wrong, snow melts. Power lines can be restrung. But damn if the building comes down in a topple or a highway collapses in a pile of rubble and yellow school buses, and none of them fixes are all that great.

But lately it seems that California is taking hits from every side that go way beyond God playing with his Bachmann® Union Pacific® Steam Digital train set. I mean, this is clearly revenge for some wrong, either electing Arnold Schwarzenegger to Governor, or the Anaheim Angels ripping off the good name of L.A. or The O.C. Whatever it is, something has gone dreadfully wrong over there, and all of a sudden, driving to work in 10 feet of visibility where I can barely see over the hood of my car and snow flurries are in a flying frenzy in front of my windshield like bouncing neutrons in the gravitational field (okay, so I really have no idea what that means) with the wind chill factor in the negative digits is nothing compared to living in California.

If it isn't mudslides and storm warnings, it's rampant fires and neighborhood evacuations. It's Santa Ana winds sweeping in from the desert to wreck havoc on San Diego, and $4.50 per gallon of gas in Modesto. If it's not wildfires, it's flash flooding. If I see one more damn "Come Work in California" commercial, I'm going to poke both my eyes out with a butter knife.

Who the hell wants to live in California anyway? Consider that:

The state has one damn foot submerged into a recession. The unemployment rate is expected to rise to 6.1 percent in 2008 and stay there for at least another year out. Most of those jobs will come out of the construction and financial industries, and if you read between the lines, that is a direct result of a dismal housing market. (This might a case of the chicken or the egg.)

Gas prices have leveled out at $3.36 per gallon. That's an average, not a high. And it's only slightly less than a full dollar above the cost of a gallon of gas this time last year (again, an average, if you live in any city, you've been paying more than that since 2001) with no relief in sight.

California is the number one spot to offload women and girls who are forced into labor and sex for hire. (I can't make this stuff up.) At least 18 countries contribute to the California labor force through human trafficking, according to the latest research by U.C. Berkeley. And, I swear, the state expects to declare January 11 as National Human Trafficking Day, but only in California.

Barry Bonds wants to play next season. Just ask Michael Vick how you stay in shape in prison.

Speaking of, California leads the nation in the number of inmates who have been released on parole or probation. That's 5 million, um citizens, living in the state. Another 200,000 or so are still in prison awaiting their almost certain release because the system is overcrowded and many prisons are operating at critical capacity. That's a fancy term for they're fucked. (It's also defined as being around double capacity, or 10,500 for a facility intended for less than 6,000.) The good news? Prisons are actually less crowded than last year. The bad news? It's not because there are less criminals. (All joking aside, a small percentage of inmates are actually transferred out of state but remain incarcerated.)

Most Californians have never heard of FIOS. (Okay, I just had to throw that one in there.)

A recent study of the California wildfires found local residents were exposed to substantial health risk from the ash, which increased the presence of caustic metals in the local ecosystems (that's rainwater runoff, drinking water supplies and the ground.) People are being poisoned by traces of arsenic, lead and copper. But what help for it? Gloves, long-sleeve shirts (and pants,) frequent showers and a dust mask. Because I'm sure everyone just has a supply in their medicine cabinet (or will from now on.) Good luck with that whole groundwater thing by the way.

At least State Farm will always be there for you.

It seems like every month or so the report of some new catastrophe, some man-made, some the wrath of God, comes out of California. With a spiraling cost of living, fault lines, and the Sacramento Kings, it's hard to come up with a plausible argument for why anyone lives there.

Oh, I know the usual answer. It's always sunny in California (oh wait, that's Philadelphia.) But does relatively mild temperatures (which doesn't apply to the state north of San Francisco anyway) make up for all the life-threatening happenings of which earthquakes really are the least of your worries? I mean, have you been to San Bernardino? It makes Baltimore look as statistically safe as Disneyland. There has to be something that draws people there and keeps them there besides the weather and an $8.00 an hour state minimum wage.

I don't get it myself. But I'll take snow storms and potholes any day.

From: Andrew Marx
To: dshifrer
Subject: Early Gift/Late Gift
Date: Tue, 27 Nov 2007

Hi Dara,

So I wanted to give you your Christmas gift early because by the time I send you the CD I am going to make for your birthday, it's going to be Christmas - if that made any sense.

Here is a partial tracklist for the cd

2. 'Lake Michigan' Rogue Wave

8. 'Won't Go Home Without You' Maroon 5

9. 'Car Crash' Matt Nathanson

15. 'Into the Hollow' Queens of the Stone Age

Andy

From: Dara Shifrer
To: amarx
Subject: RE: Early Gift/Late Gift
Date: Thu, 29 Nov 2007

I do look forward to the mix.

Thank you.

So how was the Thanksgiving? Since you haven't complained, I imagine that there were no disasters. I actually had a lot of fun and that's generally not my practice on Thanksgivings of late. A friend and I planned an impromptu party the night before - he's a very good cook and made really delicious enchiladas and guacamole and stuff - maybe 5 people showed up but they had a very good time which made me have a good time. Then the enchilada cooker and I got into a spat because he wants to date me and I refuse. I am physically attracted to him but know he's not good dating material - if I were 23 maybe... he plays guitar very well... was involved in the music industry... blah blah blah. Plus I love Michael forever! Forever! ;-)

Speaking of 23, one of the girls in my program is 23 and I invited her over on Thanksgiving because I knew she wasn't doing anything. Her 23-ness is excruciating to me. I hadn't realized how old I had gotten until spending time with one so young. So flippant about life, about her behavior,... it's painful I guess because I remember being like that. She came over for dinner last night and off-handedly reported her first lesbian experience <eye roll> of two weeks ago. She has this incredibly dramatic i.e. ridiculous love life with three men. And she's this beautiful little girl with long brown curls smoking, drinking... oh well, she'll grow up.

I'm going to switch over to your other email.

From: Andrew Marx
To: dshifrer
Subject: RE: Early Gift/Late Gift
Date: Thu, 29 Nov 2007

TG was sedate. I was on my own for three days because my mom just started a new position and only had Thurs/Fri off. There are two shopping centers in either direction from her house, about equidistant, twenty minutes of walking, so one day I went one direction and the next day I went the other direction. It was nice, in the sixties the sun mostly shining. TG itself was nothing special, just dinner with my mom and some friends (who always seem to know me better than I know them) and my aunt and uncle. My uncle is entertaining. He'll say something really intelligent and thought-provoking, and then repeat it verbatim until you cut him off or distract him with baked goods.

I think you should date the guy even if he isn't source material. Secondary sources are just as good - no matter what intellectual snobbery says. Wikipedia rules!

From: Dara Shifrer
To: amarx
Subject: RE: Four Beers and I'm Andy
Date: Thu, 29 Nov 2007

Hmmm. I have no New Year's plans which is fine by me. Well, I do have one plan, to not be in Apple Valley. I need to stop being mean to my family. You know I love them right? I had been agonizing over buying my Christmas ticket and finally bought it on Sunday morning. Then got a call that my Grandma had had a heart attack that morning. My mom comes from a big family (six kids) and my grandma/her mom comes from a big family (5 sisters and 1 brother). So one of my uncles is calling everybody to tell them and he tells my grandma's sister, who is also old and dementia-ed, so she calls everybody in that generation and tells them that my grandma had died...

So my uncle had to call people back and say no no just a heart attack...

But then, come Monday, she died. So he had to make all of those phone calls again...

My grandma had not been herself for some five years so it's not a sad thing. But it's interesting to me to watch all of the family drama instantly unfold. One uncle is in Thailand for a long-anticipated vacation and sent the family an email saying that "Mom would have wanted me to travel on..." which I thought was somewhat obnoxious even if he did make the right choice. So when to have the funeral. Where. Point is I might be at a funeral over Christmas which is fine by me because it would be a much more efficient use of my family time.

In other news, my birthday was pretty fair. I was suffering from diabetes and melanoma and general life exhaustion. Luckily the doctors have decided that I will live. Michael and I had been going to therapy for last several months because he loves me but can't commit to me. Ech. And it pretty much winded down unsuccessfully the week before my birthday but I can't complain about it to anybody b/c the situation is so ridiculous but my body complained all on its own and I developed several life-threatening diseases and a total aversion to work. So that has passed. I wasn't going to do anything for my birthday because that's how I like it generally but my friend Casidy's sister's husband died in a freak car accident. He was 27 and had a 1 1/2 year old baby so it was pretty shocking and of course a reminder that life is precious and should be lived with a vengeance. So I ended up spending the evening at Casidy's house on my birthday before he left to go to the funeral.

I am fascinated by this brother in Nebraska. Why? Why would he go there? Wasn't he a happy jolly kid before? I met him and remember him being a music/drama guy or am I confusing brothers?

Well and there's an email for you!

Dara

From: Andrew Marx
To: dshifrer
Subject: Christmas Time Again
Date: Sun, 2 Dec 2007

Love the Christmas show I went to last night. The only lack of serenity was the drunken couples in the row in front of me, but they were easier to ignore towards the end of the show and there were some gorgeous renditions.

On my brother, well look, he dropped out of a two-year school in a family of underachievers who nevertheless probably were perceived as being very successful (at least insofar as college was concerned) from his perspective. He finally rebelled and moved as far away from his parental units as possible (not unlike all three of his siblings, I might add) though he added the wrinkle of converting to Christianity and got baptized and so at the end of all things, he moves to Nebraska. Where in there, I ask you, is really the worst offense?

I think my brother really needed to make decisions on his own, feel loved and just do something that wouldn't put him in the line of fire anymore. He accomplished all three and since I have nothing to say to him and he doesn't respond to outreach, we leave it at that. (Of course, lest you think me unkind, I don't really communicate with anyone in my family these days. It's just my brother takes it personally whereas my other sibs do not).

We had snow Sunday night. Unfortunately, it snowed for an hour and then froze and then it rained overnight so everything turned to slush. It was in the thirties by the time I left for work, so it was easy enough to clean off, but not much fun to play in. I heard 'snow storm' for today, but the sun is shining and there is distinctly not a trace of storm anywhere I can see. I just checked. It's been downgraded to flurries. Very disappointing.

Andrew

From Concert-Central.com
Sister Hazel, Somerville Theatre, Somerville, MA December 1, 2007
Review by Andrew

So there are very few bands that could get me to come out for a concert on a "12 Days of Christmas Tour" but Sister Hazel just happens to be one of them. Sister Hazel's last radio hit (well, only radio hit) "All for You" was 10 years ago, but the band has been active with tours and new albums despite the lack of mainstream support, including their first holiday album Santa's Playlist. In 2000, I saw them at a fans-only radio show at Sunset Station Casino in Las Vegas and I was blown away. The four guys Ken Block, Andrew Copeland, Jett Beres and Ryan Newell (along with drummer Mark Trojanowski) all sing vocals and their harmonies are transcendent. Their musicianship is stellar and I almost thought, almost thought they could pull off a Christmas show that I would enjoy.

Rock versions of Christmas songs, and lots of them, but Sister Hazel found a balance between their southern rock roots and unique interpretations of traditional Christmas tunes. They brought a unique flavor to "White Christmas" (a full reggae version and an acappella version during a stunning rendition of "River") and a convincing bluegrass rendition of "The Dreidel Song" which prompted Block and Copeland to trade "Dueling Banjos" briefly. Christmas Time Again became a rollickin' tongue-in-cheek rap song complete with Beres in fully blinged Santa Claus gear.

From: Dara Shifrer
To: amarx
Subject: RE: Christmas Time Again
Date: Mon, 3 Dec 2007

I'm in the throes of finals for the next week or so...

What Christmas show?

From: Andrew Marx
To: dshifrer
Subject: RE: Christmas Time Again
Date: Mon, 3 Dec 2007

Sister Hazel 12 Days of Christmas Tour. It was mostly holiday songs with some of the hits mixed in. I don't do holiday shows... well, ever. But this one seemed like a good choice.

Let me know when you resurface. I have a date with Becca in a couple of weeks. (We will meet halfway in Connecticut). She asked about you. I didn't contribute much of anything.

From Concert-Central.com
Wino Vino, Austin Figurative Gallery, Austin, TX December 7, 2007
Review by Dara

A fantastic polka-infused band in the style of Gogol Bordello and Man Man, frankly the sound is too unique to be occurring in so many bands without sounding like another rip-off, but still enjoyable, don't know if they were actually immigrants from the poor country or no-style punks

From: Andrew Marx
To: dshifrer
Subject: Snow Falling
Date: Thu, 13 Dec 2007

Oh Dara!

The main road off campus has been a parking lot since 2pm today. The one coworker who left in her car hours ago still hasn't gotten home yet. So the rest of us are basically trapped here for the time being (probably a long time). It's not bad though. The snow is very light now. They haven't plowed our parking lot yet but they will at some point. We have a TV lounge next door if it gets closer to prime time.

So now it's later and...

My 16 hour work day just ended at 11pm. Since we have one road in and out of campus, it was a parking lot for about 8 hours once the snow started falling. Some combination of everyone leaving at once, fast falling snow, and icy conditions. Even though I only had a mile and a half to go; there was no way I was going to risk getting stuck in my car for the rest of the day.

So the snow did stop completely around 10pm, and public safety let us know that the roads were clearer (and they had eventually plowed the parking lot because our cars were buried). Dinner was at the dining commons; kind of expensive and more than a little gross but it was food. The pizza was cold and burnt, not an appealing combination. Folks from my department and another drank scotch (I had three sips; it pretty much knocked me out) and watched TV and played board games in the lounge all evening. It was altogether as pleasant as being trapped at work was going to be under any occasion.

The road was frozen and chewed up so it was like driving on rocks, but it had been plowed and already well traveled. Abandoned cars (either stuck, run out of gas, or straight up abandoned) were littered on the street. Then, I got to my street and it was totally clear. My parking lot was well plowed and parking was easy peasy. Tomorrow is payday and I got my boss to agree to a dress down Friday because today sucked kaka.

The people who did try to get off campus were reporting travel times of 4 plus hours and being stuck on the road, being stuck on the Turnpike, hitting walls of other cars going nowhere. Who the hell wants to be in the car that long going nowhere?

Fun loong day. And more tomorrow.

From: Dara Shifrer
To: amarx
Subject: RE: Snow Falling
Date: Fri, 14 Dec 2007

Wow!! I haven't even heard anything about this. This isn't typical is it? I assume not since you bothered to tell the story. It sounds like fun to me - well except the 16 hours at work bit. But drinking scotch at work, eating pizza with undergrads, I don't know Andy, I bet you had a good time. Personally I am a big fan of natural disaster situations - everyone becomes animated and interacts in ways they never would otherwise. It is 80 degrees here. I lie, it's chilly and rainy, BUT it was 80 degrees earlier this week!!!

I had a Christmas party at my house last night for the people in my program. I forced them all to play games and they complained and said I was acting like a middle school teacher, which I was, it still comes out at times, but damned if they didn't behave just like middle school students. People are so funny. Age doesn't make that much difference.

From: Andrew Marx
To: dshifrer
Subject: RE: Snow Falling
Date: Sun, 16 Dec 2007

It's worse today because of the wind, and it's turning to rain which is going to freeze overnight. Good stuff. Someone in my parking lot is cleaning off cars to escape. I'm assuming it's because they are going skiing.

I can't imagine wanting to drive the streets right now because the snow clogs on your windshield and it's blowing every direction at about 40 miles per hour. And when it turns to rain, it gets slippery.

Of course, nobody has plowed our parking lot yet so they are driving through five inches of snow just to get to the street. I planned not to have to go anywhere today and did all my groceries like a good boy, so I'm planted and I got football in a few hours. I have a ton of to-do stuff for the web and writing, so I'll dive in if I feel like it.

I spent the day with Becca yesterday. We didn't talk about much of anything. It was pleasant.

I'll be in Vegas the week of 9-13 March for business. You should meet me there.

Happy Sunday!

From: Dara Shifrer
To: amarx
Subject: RE: Snow Falling
Date: Thu, 20 Dec 2007

I refrain from driving even with rain so I can't imagine the people who are risking the weather you're having. I remember meeting a woman from Minnesota and her casual tales of cars skidding off the road on a regular basis. I have apparently been spoiled in that respect.

I haven't talked to Becca in a long time. Julianna is thinking about inviting her to visit in Austin. Julianna is a much better friend than me on all respects. ;-) I am tired of people this week.

So it's not so bad to be home in California. I got in late last night and am up drinking my mom's homemade hot chocolate. The family appears to be happy so it shouldn't be a disaster like last Christmas. EXCEPT we have to get up at 3am tonight to catch a plane to go to Washington for my grandma's funeral. My mom and I fought when she made these insane plans (also insane b/c we have a 2 hour window between arrival and funeral time and then are leaving entirely after one night there) but yelling at your mom the week that her mom dies isn't a very daughterly thing to do.

I am jealous of your day of lots of groceries, football and the web. I am going to be meeting up with high school pal Catina for lunch and high school pal Amy for tea or something after lunch. I don't think you've met either of them.

I will figure out the plan for March!

:-) Dara

From: Andrew Marx
To: dshifrer
Subject: RE: Snow Falling
Date: Fri, 21 Dec 2007

Yesterday's snow fall was mostly gone by the afternoon. It rained from about 10am on and everything turned to slush and then to ice. So it was slick beyond belief this morning, but that's the worst of it. The temperature will be back in the 30's by midweek and it will be business as usual. I was inside all day yesterday and really spent a lot of the day in bed (though I was a good boy and I cleaned the 5 inches of snow off my car before it froze into a popsicle and even backed my car into the space so I would not have traction problems in the morning.) It was a mild morning today, but I started late and stopped for errands so I got to work later than my usual.

I am already ready to go home. I'm burned out with this office space right now and not even my string of Christmas lights is cheering me up. Someone made cookies though, and they are quite good.

From: Dara Shifrer
To: amarx
Subject:
Date: Thu, 27 Dec 2007

Andy,

I got home from my whirlwind trip last night and was pleasantly surprised by your mix! I quite liked it - lots of new material. It is confirmed that you will be receiving some long long overdue mixes from me very soon. Thank you for the mix!

I spent a week on the West Coast but also flew up to Washington for my grandma's funeral amidst that. It was a good visit. My middle sister is moving into her own apartment with her kids which is a HUGE step for her. My youngest sister is ga ga for a boy of 27 and fully plans to marry him which just boggles my mind, but she's far more normal than I. I am really really happy to be home. I've had a lovely day of home errands. My next project is to re-alphabetize my CDs. I have been in music mecca for the last several months - not live shows - but downloading and discovering new bands and genres.

Your sister told me that you, she and Cassie are 95% sure you're going to Vegas and I told her that I am 80% sure that I'm going too! It would be a family business/Vegas friends/Marx tour which appeals to me since I rarely make excursions for less. One conflict though is South by Southwest in Austin - but I think this opportunity to see all of you is worth more.

How is 2008 looking for you? I feel satisfied with my life. With work at least and no real desire for more than that at this time. Have you resolved your New Year's dilemma yet?

From: Andrew Marx
To: dshifrer
Subject: RE:
Date: Thu, 27 Dec 2007

Oh yes. When I was listening to your mix (I do always test the cd just to make sure it all seems to be playing) I knew it was at the top or near the top at least of one of the best I've made.

My current obsession is with about 60 songs on Vh1's best hits of the 90's. I own a small percentage of the songs on the list, and

I want a good chunk of the rest. I had to hunt down a printed listed (because on the website, you have to view them by video which is hard to make a list by) so that I can download them from iTunes.

Right now, I'm on tap to see the Dresden Dolls on Saturday. Also happens to be at the same time as the Patriots game (the last of the season, going for the 16-0 record) so I'm actually a little torn. But I'm sure the show will be exquisite drama (and the band has already sent out a message to their constituents to dress up as if for a costume party. I absolutely will not, but it will be fun anyway). Front row seats.

I'm working this week (one of the select few open offices on campus) because my boss likes to be open. Well, it's alright. Today went fast enough, and I always have something to do (though I typically push off the stuff that bores me, so that is what is to do). Just less distractions than usual - which is supposed to be a good thing.

Therefore, I will be working New Year's Eve as well. And then I was invited to the party, but my other friend is working up some other social gathering because his cousin plus new bride are in town and he agreed I wouldn't have to drive that night wherever we end up (it's like bribing me with candy).

I think my sister is set on Vegas, it's just a matter of the whens and the wheres (well, where to stay) so you should bump yours to 82%. My dad has opened his house to us to stay that week.

AM

From Concert-Central
Meow Meow The Orpheum Boston, MA December 29, 2007
Review by Andrew

Meow Meow opened the show in the audience, making her way in full winter gear (with luggage) to the front of the stage, taking an assist from the house crew to get on to stage. She then proceeded to introduce herself and undress, one piece at a time, with the help of men from the front row. Sitting almost dead center, I was asked first to help her out of her winter coat while she talked to the audience holding her mic. It was challenging because she was wearing mittens and I was trying to a) not touch her inappropriately and b) not pull her mittens off with her coat.

After depositing her jacket on the stage, she asked me to help her out of her pants. Yeah, I admit, I thought she was kidding. She bent over in front of me and then turned and asked, "Have you ever undressed a woman before?" Then she bent over with her head around her ankles. I grabbed the zipper, without ever touching her body, and then was urged to pull down on both sides of her pants to bring them down around her ankles.

At which point, she continued to struggle out of items of clothing with other people in the front row. "The male dancers usually do this," she told the crowd while wrestling out of a vest.

Her entire set was only one song. She was accompanied by keyboard player Lance Horne (an accomplished musician in his own right). It was cabaret and opera, mostly in French. She wailed and belted and crowed and engaged the audience without ever missing a beat. When she wanted the help of someone in the audience, she would admonish them "Quickly!" and even once switched to German, "Schnell!"

Finally, calling out to Horne, she asked how much time she had left. "I have to get through one song. It's on my contract." After determining there was 5 minutes left in her set, she decided she had enough time to crowd surf. She started out on the other side of the stage but decided that half of the audience wasn't a good bet and came over to our side.

I'll admit, I still thought she was joking. After helping her out of her knickers, I guess I should have known better. She made a grand show of it, even asking two young men in the third row to fill in a gap so that she could make it past the first few rows. Then she leaned out and "floated" (term used loosely) her way to the back of the house, all the while, gabbing with the audience and finishing the tune.

As remarkable as that fact was alone, even more unbelievable was that for most of her crowd surfing, she was sitting straight up with her legs split. The crowd supported her (mostly) all the way back to the stage where she collected her things and departed.

From: Andrew Marx
To: dshifrer
Subject: Undress
Date: Sun, 30 Dec 2007

I saw a performance artist last night called Meow Meow. The performer came over to me (in the front row) and asked me to help her out of her jacket (because she was holding the mic in one hand) and then asked me to unzip her pants. I honestly thought she was kidding and went to sit down. She proceeded to bend over so her head was around her ankles and I unzipped her pants and then gently pulled them down by my fingers until they were around her ankles (she had someone else pull them off completely).

I added a "Performance" category to the concert website. And "Gypsy" under "World Music."

From: Dara Shifrer
To: amarx
Subject: RE: Undress
Date: Wed, 2 Jan 2008

I thought you had already seen the Dresden Dolls!?! I think their music is okay but I really like their appearance. See we had this exact conversation already!

Well that Meow Meow show definitely warrants a new category. I have definitely never had a similar experience though I feel that I ought to seek it out now... Didn't you feel special to have been the audience member chosen?

I would be interested in staying at your father's house if that works out. I think a hotel is out for me - I would probably beg nights at old friends' house - I don't know - we'll see how it works out. I am excited though! The tentative plan is to go to Utah to see my dad's relatives the first part of the week (while you're working) and then spend time with you and Megan the first part of your actual vacation.

I was up at 530am from the guilt of not having done any work the last two days though I suppose it wasn't as big of a sin as I felt. My New Year's was interesting I suppose, though not meaningful and not boding well for the rest of the year. ;-) I liked Julianna's statement that anything can happen in 365 days - so much possibility - though I believe she is mad at me again and as usual. ;-) To avoid unsavory boys and in tribute to recent resolution of tension, she and I went to a shady bar for a bit where I met a former math teaching, bartending guy who is now pursuing comedy - had lived in CA, LV, etc. - interesting and forward but lack of tenure is suspect. The cover charges for downtown were anywhere from $10-125 - usually free to $15 - so we chose on the lesser end - a bling party that called for big tacky jewelry. I was embarrassed that I had so much tack on hand and had worn it sincerely not so long ago. In accordance with my worst fears, it was swarming with early 20 somethings. So, in the end, the unsavory boys saved us and picked us up and we ended up at a party of semi-friends. Semi- because I knew the hosts but usually attend their nerdier parties. This was a group of 'burners' - people in Austin who fancy themselves as making it their practice to live in the ethos of Burning Man (art festival extravaganza in northern Nevada every year) on a daily basis. I met, for example, Forest, a Christian chiropractor. They're fairly annoying people but enjoyable to watch at least. Where did you go and what did you do?

All right, the sun is rising so I must be heading to the shower!!

And I hear my cat fighting outside!!

From: Andrew Marx
To: dshifrer
Subject: RE: Undress
Date: Wed, 2 Jan 2008

Yeah I saw Dresden Dolls in June. I would go again anytime. They are entertaining and I'm starting to recognize some of the songs.

New Year's was at a billiards club that did a big food spread and every group got a pool table, dj music, champagne. It was alright, but as soon as I stopped drinking, I kind of fell flat. It was fun, though the dj was remarkably annoying (I don't think they should be allowed to speak) and I got over playing pool after about two games. So that left eating (yay!) drinking (mostly yay!) and watching college boys (yay!)

My brother is in town now, though dinner tonight is pretty much it before they leave. Then I go back to a semi-normal work/life routine. Although it's playoff football so that shall consume me for a few weekends.

From Concert-Central.com
Black Joe Lewis, Emo's, Austin, TX January 4, 2008
Review by Dara

A testament to the diversity and quality that my favorite venue was offering for free week, chaos ensued from this point on but it was a string of be-horned guys doing funk-blues, possibly in a line and stepping in unison as if it were 1965.

Title: What do you say to the DJ?

---- Original Message ----
From: Dara Shifrer
To: amarx
Subject: RE: Concert Site
Date: Sat, 15 Mar 2008

and cover band!

From Concert-Central.com
O'Death, Hole in the Wall, Austin, TX March 15, 2008
Review by Dara

My favorite band of South by Southwest - they almost made me cry, so unique and perfect taking the darkest country and wacking it up, think the guy's voice is big part of their charm - unique - though disappointed by his youth and cleanliness but these are things that cannot be helped, maybe a tad of gypsy there too, also can't help that they're from New York, I remember the fiddler doing a superb job too.

9

Chapter Nine *When I Go To Heaven*

---- Original Message ----
From: Andrew Marx
To: dshifrer
Subject: When I Go to Heaven
Date: Fri, 11 Jan 2008

Dara, I just got your package of amazing mix cds! I think there are only like four artists I've heard of which is great. I'm excited to hear the rest (and continuously amazed at the breadth of your band-ledge compared to mine).

I've been told Regina Spektor is (or did?) playing nearby, but I don't know who she is. She's on the mix, so I guess that will give me a clue at least.

I'll have to figure out some organized way to listen to it all. Tomorrow morning is a project day for me (writing stuff) so that's when I will hear at least one disc. But then it's football from 4pm Saturday until 8pm on Sunday, so I pretty much drop everything and plant myself in front of the TV (it's what I want to do when I go to Heaven).

Someday soon, I keep promising myself to go on the mother of all cd-spending sprees (you know, while they still sell cds) but honestly, a lot of stores have just stopped stocking discs these days. I have to direct-order 1/2 of my bands from their own websites. It makes the whole cd shopping experience less thrilling, and don't get me started on the lack of tactile enjoyment of shopping on Amazon.

Our break ended at work and I zoomed into craziness that won't stop until commencement. It makes the semester fly by. June will be here in the blink of an eye.

From Concert-Central.com
Flatfoot 56, Red 7, Austin, TX January 12, 2008
Review by Dara

Heather Rae's lover Shannon was playing bass - odd to see him out of his cowboy hat and in punk mode, the lead singer was a crowd motivator and maneuvered some kind of red-sea-divide of the crowd though with no purpose that I could see, joyous and young, even some half-hearted crowd diving.

From: Dara Shifrer
To: amarx
Subject: RE: When I Go to Heaven
Date: Mon, 14 Jan 2008

Oh, be still my mix-making heart. You are the sweetest of sweethearts! Sorry if I made you gag. But when you said that you have to figure out an organized way to listen, I just kleptzed...

All I know of Regina Spektor is that she is from Europe or thereabouts, maybe Russia? She played with The Strokes but is primarily a solo artist. I particularly like that song because she sings the lyrics "little bag of cocaine, little bag of cocaine" so inappropriately cutely.

I am shocked every time you tell me that you like football and this time was no different. Here's something to dissuade you: Texans love football! Is this who you want to associate with!?!

CDs. I am very intrigued by what is going on with the music industry. I am a shameless non-royalty-paying peer-to-peer downloader. If I disappear, please tell my family it was because I exposed my crimes in this email. I used to buy CDs like they were Snickers bars but I have not bought one in years, years, years. They're so expensive! They take up so much room! But it breaks my heart that the music I have collected since 2000 is not properly catalogued and displayed. And these people who store all of their music in mp3 format drive me crazy. At least I burn CDs... but clearly things are changing. I've read several articles stating that the music industry needs to stop whining and catch up with the technological changes. And have heard that bands really make their money from tours and merchandise rather than CDs. I would never never have explored so much music if I had to buy CDs to hear it. But all of this does not take away from the fact that these artists should be paid for their music. Please discuss.

So how does 2008 stand at this early point?

From: Andrew Marx
To: dshifrer
Subject: RE: When I Go to Heaven
Date: Tue, 15 Jan 2008

Well, so far, things have gotten much further on the Vegas plans. Friends are driving in / flying in to meet us. I heard a rumor that my dad and wife are coming up for the weekend. I really want some non-parent time with Megan. Megan, however, is of the opinion that it doesn't matter if they are around because they are self-entertaining.

I agree with you completely about music, but I disagree about CDs. I don't buy CDs unless I'm dedicated to the artist because I think the visual element isn't strong enough on its own. However, I consider the CD a way to register my support for the artist (like voting in the election). Artists make nothing on their music (except in limited cases when they get an advance from the record company) which is why they don't care two squats about downloading, and the progressive artists are actively giving it away. Even though I know most of their revenue is t-shirts (and to a lesser extent, the concerts themselves) I cannot bring myself to buy one most of the time. I always look, but I'm usually not interested.

I really like the new Radiohead album. Never thought I would say that.

I buy tracks one at a time. I hear something I like and go find it on iTunes. It's a little more expensive, but it's one of those things that counts to the record companies. I don't do anything in illegal downloading, but as far as I can tell, it's all the rage among my friends...I don't know. I don't mind paying for it, but buying the whole album: not unless I've heard it first.

So there's the catch: I won't pay for it unless I've already heard it but how do I get exposed to it if pop music is so narrow that the same four artists are on the radio all the time? I guess that's where opening acts and iTunes free downloads and friends' mix cds come in.

I think most pop music is atrocious. I like that you send me all sorts of reasonably obscure stuff. It makes me feel more cultured.

From Concert-Central.com
Friends of Dean Martinez, Hole in the Wall, Austin, TX January 16, 2008
Review by Dara

Pleasant surprise because have had their CD courtesy of BestGirlfriend's ExHusband for years and have always liked it, reminiscent of my personal gods: Godspeed You! Black Emperor, found their live show captivating though may have just been suiting my mood, baseball-hatted man crouched over his pedal steel and glancing at a laptop (the source of the undertone of wind and drone I guess) convinced me of the versatility of the pedal steel by making it whine and wail in ways very counter to last band, accompanied by a drummer who managed to make his slow slightly off-kilter tempo look intense, basically a more ambient version of the proggy psych-metal that I really enjoy, I spent the set daydreaming about the darkness that must inhabit these two men, they're probably frat boys.

From: Dara Shifrer
To: amarx
Subject: RE: When I Go to Heaven
Date: Tue, 22 Jan 2008

The best conversation I've had this week has been with Crahobi (my cat). I keep catching myself murmuring to myself and making odd noises that would be totally inappropriate if there was actually someone else to hear it, which my neighbor probably does. Moreover, my skin is flaking off because it is so cold, both of which persuade me to be more of a hermit. My stomach and intestines are just not right. I would blame it on the mounds of spinach leaves I've been eating, but my nose is stuffed too. I have been typing so much that my hands ache at night. I am developing little OCD twitches like taking obsessive amounts of notes on articles and picking lint off my carpeting as I walk back and forth to the bathroom. My point is that I'm going insane. At least you know if they come to you with questions. Sex or alcohol would solve every single one of these problems but when I'm insane like this, I refrain from all - now I wonder which is really causing which...

I'm glad that we see eye to eye on the music but I don't understand how we digress on CDs? You probably don't remember by now. I guess you meant that by paying for tracks on iTunes you are getting the musician their due notice? I know you're right. Music wipes away all my ethics. Or making little gestures within such a giant game seems meaningless to me.

So I'm reading a really enjoyable book that I think you would also enjoy, though he sometimes needs to lose his little shtick (I have no idea how to spell it). P.J. O'Rourke. I feel like I already told you this as I am writing it. He used to write for Rolling Stone but wrote a novel Holidays in Hell detailing his adventures as a journalist in third world countries. I think there is an element of bleeding heart to him BUT (don't stop listening) it is all masked and bundled up in wry non-PC offensive humor. There's also stuff about his travels within the US - a paragraph on a skirmish between activist Harvard students and Harvard alumnus made me laugh out loud.

Well, I am off to my oil painting class - also a symptom that belongs in the first paragraph.

Happy that it's much colder where you are than where I am,
Dara

From Concert-Central.com
Nanosmash, Carousel Lounge, Austin, TX February 7, 2008
Review by Dara

Anticipation built as they set up a mess of gear and wound sparkly lights around the microphone, the red glittery moog guitar player was dressed in red elf clothing and then took off his red jacket to reveal a red "Flash" t-shirt and put on historical pilot goggles, the lead vocalist came in his plaid pajama pants and leftover eyeliner from the night before, the drummer was a preppy slightly effeminate man and the electric guitarist was a squat metalist likely from San Antonio, they were sci-fi punk with departures into pretty average rock, the red man gave "spooky" narratives through a voice distorter that were often too quiet to discern, the electric guitarist played riffs that ought to have been a lot quieter, seemed like a band with a concept with potential but really poor sound management.

From: Andrew Marx
To: dshifrer
Subject: Band Name
Date: Tue, 12 Feb 2008

What kind of mp3 player do you use? Is it an iPod? I actually really like my iPod (the super small one, but I just load my favorite tracks only and then I basically know everything on there is good).

I can't remember if I told you, but disc 5 is by far my favorite of the ones you sent me, though that is subject to change as I get to know the other discs. Our music sharing is a little antiquated, I guess (though I still use the cds in my car routinely; I don't listen to the radio except sports news). I don't know, we should have some portal for sharing mp3 files (though I guess that's illegal, isn't it? Funny how the simplest ideas...) Do you rip the tracks I send you into mp3s? I've been meaning to with the discs you sent me, but I haven't yet. I just play the discs at home on my shitty cd player and then graduate them to the car when I'm ready. (It's very ceremonial and all).

I've been sick and my heat hasn't been on; they have to replace a valve, right when it's single digit temperatures outside. I don't think that helped my feeling better much. But mostly, I think things are less frantic, at least for a few weeks coming up. It's been snowing a lot lately, but in piddly amounts. More on the way and then washed away by rain. I'm looking forward to Vegas. It seems to be the only time we see each other. When is South by Southwest? Are you able to come to Vegas and see some shows too?

Andy

From SmartReMarx.com
Friday B.S.: Complex Reality March 14, 2008
Posted by Andrew

After a two-year estrangement, I finally boarded the plane to take me back to the mother country. Granted, we boarded two hours after our departure time, but the pilot assured us that we would make up the time in the air. Before the wheels touch down again, the rolling hills of lights greet you from every direction. On the right side of the plane, you can see a glimmer of green, a sheen of the Manhattan skyline (albeit, buildings draped in faded pastels), the crystalline spire of light arching into the sky from the peak of a pyramid of glass. And...hey, what the hell are those three buildings?

Welcome to Las Vegas, a city that is ever-transforming itself at the forefront of American consumerism. From what the masses want to what they don't know that they want yet. And damnit, it's blocking my view.

The newest trend in Las Vegas is the dual sisters the condo complex and the timeshare tower. It's disturbing to see the rise of the high rise along the Strip skyline. In fact, (and I can't claim to even know who owns the properties) there are three sister towers that now completely obstruct the view of the Strip from the Bellagio to the Mirage from the west-facing direction (which also happens to be the direction you are looking if you sit on the right side of the plane peering out the window). MGM has a residential tower, so does Trump. On the northern corner of the Strip, there are new construction projects between the Riveria and the Sahara (admittedly, traditionally a stretch of undeveloped space) and a Hilton homes property across the street and another condo complex owned by whomever.

A megaresort, itself a hub of residential activity, is being built where the Stardust and Wayne Newton once reigned. More and more, every square inch of development space along Las Vegas Boulevard is...well, being developed. But it's no longer just hotel expansions (except for Encore, the new Wynn tower and the seemingly endless expansion of Caesar's Palace). And it's not just on the Strip either. There are towers being built in every corner of town. Out by the Rampart Casino in Summerlin, a 25-story residential complex is ready to open. Reserve a unit with a Strip view.

The net effect of all this development brings up a curious question: who the hell is going to live there? With timeshares, it seems reasonable to think they could sell enough units to find the venture profitable. And if you weren't planning on living there full-time anyway, it probably makes sense to seek out a property along the Strip where the action is a little closer. Presumably, the Strip towers come with a certain level of amenity, be it dedicated parking lots, laundry service or grocery delivery. The condominiums are a different consideration though. So for most people, are they are a second home? Do you get some resale value from owning the property? (I honestly can't imagine that's the case just given how saturated the market is with similar options). How many people seriously consider using their unit in Sky Las Vegas (next to Circus Circus) as a primary residence? Can you rent them out profitably?

Look, I'm not foolish enough to think that the developers would build as much as they have without a plan for profit. So someone obviously thinks these properties are the winning play. And I can see the appeal of living on the Las Vegas Strip as kind of a status choice. Though according to one sales pitch, condo conversions "are providing a lower cost alternative to single family homes." Are you kidding? Maybe condos near Nellis Air Force base are the lower cost alternative, but $1 million plus high rise condos on Las Vegas Boulevard? The MGM Mirage City Center Las Vegas condos which are described as "Manhattan-value apartments that...will attract retired baby boomers seeking a low-maintenance lifestyle, celebrities, and the rich"? And even if it was cheaper than buying a single-family home, what slipshod parent would raise their three kids, ages 4, 10 and 12 on the Strip?

The megaresorts (of which there are two in development that I know of) are truly the most audacious of all. The concept is a self-enclosed environment where you never have to leave to shop, eat, gamble, piss, poop or park. MGM Mirage's City Center complex? 2 boutique hotels, 2,500 residential units, and 550,000 square feet of retail space. And that's just what hasn't been built yet. The MGM already has the main hotel and the Signature, which is the condo hotel tower. Not to mention MGM Mirage owns most of the hotels on the southern-half of the Strip to begin with.

It's disconcerting to see the landscape of the city change to something I don't understand. It bothers me that depending on where you stand, your view of that famous skyline is disrupted by a grossly distorted new urban reality. But Las Vegas was always built for dreamers. The developers who take the next logical step in consumer development, the salesmen who convince us that this is exactly the kind of project that was built just for each and every one of us, and the dreamers themselves, taken in by the romantic notion that yeah, maybe someday this will be right for me, and buy into the entire fantasy. I haven't reached the point where I dread flying back, but I think it has finally sunk in that gazing out on to the city as the plane touches down will never be the same again.

From Concert-Central.com
Jay Reatard, Beerland, Austin, TX March 15, 2008
Review by Dara

My beloved lead singer of Lost Sounds, his look fit his irreputable reputation: face never breaking free from the cover of his shaggy hair, he was younger than I would have imagined, he was

also a lot more intense and together than I would have imagined, he knows his music up and down and left and right, this
reincarnation sounded little like Lost Sounds (no synth, less dark
and less intense) but was some amalgam of hair metal, punk and
garage - veering from head-banging joy to darker undertone,
always fast and ferocious but light-hearted and sincere, his voice
also altered dramatically even within one song to the point that
I suspect he may be the male and female lead I hear in Lost
Sounds, may be schizophrenic but a music genius I think, Jay
and the guitarist's (also mop top curls) dedicated head-banging
was very amusing for some reason.

From Concert-Central.com
Oreskaband, Emo's (Junior), Austin, TX March 15, 2008
Review by Dara

So darling the crowd could hardly stand it, 6-piece female ska
group from Japan, all energy and high-skill, didn't speak English
except for a few tag shout-outs for the crowd, the top crowd
response of every band I saw this year at SXSW - inspired an
inspired mosh pit, I personally think it was more the novelty of
gender and nation than the actual music, plus ska is just fun.

From: Dara Shifrer
To: amarx
Subject: Concert Site
Date: Sat, 15 Mar 2008

Could we add 'swing' and 'lounge' to the concert site?

From: Andrew Marx
To: dshifrer
Subject: RE: Concert Site
Date: Wed, 19 Mar 2008

What category are these subs of? (Sorry it took so long. In addition to sleep deprivation, I never got to my e-mail yesterday). I have a report to edit and turn in today and I can't bring myself to focus. More for distraction than anything else, I'm looking at the new reviews you posted.

Anyway, I'm going to take a wild stab with these new category adds. Let's see how I do. All three have been added.

I'm very disorganized. It's kind of funny. Back into the old routine.

From: Andrew Marx
To: dshifrer
Subject: Since My Return
Date: Wed, 19 Mar 2008

So Dara, it doesn't sound like you will object to my category classifying.

The rest of the Vegas trip was good. My friend Caitlin and I swapped shopping-time for gambling-time and she made bank. She might have complained about how much time we spent gambling (though it was equal to the amount of time I spent waiting outside Ann Taylor like a puppy) but she went home with

$200 in her pockets. I ended up with about $600 all thanks to Caitlin's picking slot machines (though she wouldn't play them). So it turned out to be a nice way to end the weekend (and the parents left Saturday!)

We got to see a runway show at the Fashion Show Mall - I didn't get a good photo of the runway itself, but it rises from the floor just before the show starts. The shows only run on the weekends, but I ended up seeing the same show (a swimwear preview) on Friday and again on Saturday because we ended up at the mall twice that weekend. Girls and their shopping.

My father left with the dogs on Saturday. His visit worked out in the end better than I could have expected. We went to birthday dinner for him at Roy's. The food was very good and the waiter played to our group perfectly. Old age has mellowed my father, so he's more fun to be around. My sister convinced him to take us to Costco, and then he proceeded to buy enough food to feed Summerlin. He's not gambling anymore.

At the Vegas airport, some legally blind guy got off the plane and couldn't find his caregiver. He was shouting at the top of his lungs for her. I don't know if she was never on the plane to begin with, or if she left him there. Either way, it was kind of sad and uncomfortable.

I had a layover in JFK but it worked out because I had some stuff I wanted to read and dinner was nice and unrushed at some bar in the terminal. I'm not saying gourmet, but it worked out. I also had coffee from a shop called Aunt Butchies. Yeah.

From Concert-Central.com
They Might Be Giants Somerville Theatre Somerville, MA March 28, 2008
Review by Andrew

Although they were out promoting a new album, the new songs were few and far between. Maybe for the couple hundred fans crammed into the Somerville Theatre, that's just as well. They played the old tracks with a pretty hard rock emphasis going all the way back to She's An Angel and Ana Ng, and the crowd ate it up. But even the new stuff was well received, the track Contrecoup got the same level of cheer as Alphabet of Nations (which, in this humble reviewer's opinion, was a major highlight.) They got the crowd going with favs like Doctor Worm, Particle Man and a rousing participation-required run through of Clap Your Hands. Both The Guitar and Hey Mr. DJ sounded more cohesive live than their studio versions (you're a real song, Pinocchio!)

Midway through the show, they shot confetti out from a cannon and again as the show closed. It was a lot, and some of it ended up on my bedroom floor.

From: Andrew Marx
To: dshifrer
Subject: Coming Attractions
Date: Thu, 3 Apr 2008

I hit the "shouldn't have gotten up at 4am" wall about 5 minutes ago and I'm reasonably sure I've been staring at my screen since then. I've spent all morning figuring out plans for my friend Jack's bachelor party in Vegas. Not that I'm organizing it, but mostly because he thinks I'm the Vegas expert (as if I know anything about strippers and night clubs). I'm humoring him. I did finally get through all of my work e-mails and I'm trying to figure out the best way to spend the rest of my work day. I have a ton of stuff I want to catch up on the websites, but I haven't been making tons of progress on anything much since my return.

I haven't been sleeping long or well lately so I have these periods of total drag during the day, but not consistently or anything.

Well anyway, it's neither here nor there. Since the sun is shining and the weather is warmer, everything is coming up roses.

I have some decent concerts coming up, REM and a few others.

From: Dara Shifrer
To: amarx
Subject: RE: Coming Attractions
Date: Fri, 4 Apr 2008

Why are you not sleeping well? I had a few poor-sleep nights this week but the reason is definitely stress. I slept well last night and am on a high because of the contrast from the rest of the week. I also got a minorly nerve-wracking conference presentation out of the way yesterday.

So I was sitting on my couch this morning reading for my class at 10am, aye, aye. When I hear raindrops which was odd enough.

Then it started raining in earnest. One of those hot-weather flash thunderstorms that make it a point to visit Texas. Then I hear these odd DINGs - and they're only occasional and in various parts of the neighborhood, but then there's DINGs all over the place and it's hail!!! Real live hail. My first solid experience with it. These balls were fully golf-ball size!! I took pictures. It ended and went back to being 70 degrees and mild. I haven't checked my car yet so maybe I won't think it such a thrilling experience this afternoon.

The thing is Andy, the concerts you go to are 'events,' and they require a lot more money, time, and general investment. The shows I see are down the street, often free and just generally low maintenance. I go in spurts, though, in terms of how much music I'm seeing. It greatly depends on being coerced by other people who don't feel as busy as I generally do. I love the shows but they wear me out pretty quickly. Especially because they all run between 10pm and 2am - you'd think nobody in Austin has a day job. Shows during the week were an impossibility when I was a teacher, but I'm trying to take advantage of my flexible schedule as a grad student and see more while I still live here.

So do you like REM live? I hate some of their stuff but I love enough of it that I was really excited to see them at this one festival. But Stipes was so obnoxiously pretentious I couldn't take it - I had also been out in the sun for an entire day and may have been overly judgmental.

;-) Dara

From *Concert-Central.com*
Cruiserweight, Stubb's, Austin, TX April 4, 2008
Review by Dara

Pop punk verging on emo, liked them but they're weird - kept suspecting they're a Christian band, three are siblings, lead singer is very attractive clean girl who is a natural performer, she wore hot shorts, they're like the band your high school friends put together (if you're a girl)

From: Dara Shifrer
To: amarx
Subject: RE: Since My Return
Date: Fri, 4 Apr 2008

Oh, and I'd been meaning to ask what you had decided to do for your friend's bachelor party? I think bachelor parties, baby showers, wedding showers, etc. are all terrible. If you have any discretion in the matter, make it good!

The blind guy story is horrible. I was walking home last night from a brief happy hour and passed an Asian kid with a backpack (college student) who was near stumbling with a non-seeing look in his guy. I assumed he was drunk and ignored him, but it struck me that he might have been having a diabetic episode and I might have been the only person who could have saved him. And I felt kind of badly... Americans are known for being non-helping-walk-on-by kind of people, or so my Egyptian friend tells me...

From: Andrew Marx
To: dshifrer
Subject: RE: Since My Return
Date: Sat, 5 Apr 2008

The plan is leaning towards a strip club but it may be a stripper in the hotel room. I just think of CSI when I imagine a stripper coming up to the hotel room. It seems like a potential for murder, or a Duke Lacrosse team-like incident. A lot of gambling and we (at least as of now) are planning on going to some restaurant/bar in Mandalay Bay. I forget which one we ended up on.

I love REM live. The only show of theirs that I didn't like was the week before the election and Michael Stipe was really depressed about Bush or something and it was just weird - the whole show was weird. But when I saw them in '03, it was magic. The new album is stellar - my friend of 25 years and I keep writing one liner e-mails to each other about the new album. Our bonding time.

Excited tonight about seeing Margaret Cho. I still wish I had the time to see some of the smaller club shows - maybe I can make that my goal for my next life.

From Concert-Central.com
Margaret Cho, Orpheum Theatre, Boston, MA April 5, 2008
Review by Andrew

I Love Margaret Cho. She comes across as very down to earth like she's your best friend. Even standing on stage in front of hundreds of people, she managed to make the show seem like a conversation in your living room. Granted, you're talking about her menstrual cycle, sex, penises, gay cruises, fag hags, P-Town, Asian stereotypes and her parents. Well, actually for some of us, that pretty much is a normal conversation in our living rooms.

From: Dara Shifrer
To: amarx
Subject: RE: Since My Return
Date: Mon, 7 Apr 2008

Oh oh oh, that's so terrible! I didn't think you would actually have to get a stripper - maybe you're excited about it though... I guess we've never discussed strippers. Male or female?

Are you seeing Margaret Cho for the second time? It's so great that you see comics. There's a comedian scene in Austin but it seems kind of expensive to me, or I just like the music too much. I don't know if you know Bill Hicks, but he started here. I adore him but he's kind of dirty and depraved. Good politics though!

Maybe I saw Stipe on a "weird" night. He seems so self-obsessed and conscious of his rock star status, but in a moanful way, similar to Mr. Morrissey. I should give him a second chance. His songs wouldn't lead me to think that of him. Oh, but that terrible song "Everybody hurts." I can't stand it Andy. Can't stand it.

I worked feverishly on a grant proposal all day and liked it! My boss is forcing me to do it but it would fund me for the next three years and is on a topic I enjoy (learning disabilities).

I usually write in the Times New Roman font but the funders require Arial and there was something really punchy, solid and satisfying about it. I might be a convert.

Dara :-)

From: Andrew Marx
To: dshifrer
Subject: RE: Since My Return
Date: Fri, 11 Apr 2008

Why would I be excited about a stripper? Going to a strip club isn't really my cup of tea. It's a guys weekend, guys hire strippers (female strippers must I point out). I fully expect that the guys will pick on me since I've never been to a Strip club and go out of their way to embarrass me with a stripper. I plan to spend the entire weekend drinking heavily so that I will come back 10 pounds heavier of liquor. I agreed to partake of a guy's weekend because that is what guys do, so I best live it up, eh? Still, guys have a weird sensibility about what passes for entertainment.

From: Dara Shifrer
To: amarx
Subject: RE: Since My Return
Date: Fri, 18 Apr 2008

I don't know why you would or wouldn't be excited about a stripper. The variation in things that excite people is pretty extreme right? Best to live it up for sure.

It is 7pm on a Friday night and I am still at school, but not minding it so much which is maybe because my social/love life is so miserably unsatisfying. ;-) I'm just winking to not sound as pathetic. We're in the very last stages of the grant we have been working on and it's kind of exciting! It's been a great learning experience that has totally eclipsed my other work for the last month.

From Concert-Central.com
Koffin Kats, Stubb's, Austin, TX May 16, 2008
Review by Dara

Worked very hard to put on a crazy show, psycho psycho-billy, guy on the huge stainless steel upright bass beat himself on the forehead with something mid-show and bled the rest of the show - possibly beat himself with a fake-blood packet - despite his seeming insanity he always concluded songs with a polite "Thank you very much for coming...," loved the multi-level multi-directional multi-colored mohawked guitarist for some reason, also impassioned and would turn profile to crowd and look up and scrunch his face up when it was time for a cappella punk or oi choruses, their stage interplay made them seem like good friends and very enjoyable show on the whole.

GOOD LOOKING

10

Chapter Ten *No, I'm Good Looking Enough*

---- Original Message ----
From: Dara Shifrer
To: amarx
Subject:
Date: Tue, 27 May 2008

Andy Marx,

I am writing for two reasons: 1) to say hello and 2) to tell you that I will be up your way at the very beginning of August. I feel petulant today because I have thrown my back out like an old lady and have been home for two days straight now which makes me a little insane. I keep imagining all of the normal people out celebrating Memorial Day at fantastic barbecues. But the truth is that it's hot as hell outside and Memorial Day has never meant anything to me. You should feel sorry for me still. ;-)

My semester ended with little fanfare. I did walk around feeling gloriously free for two whole days - envisioning healthy purpose-ful living and time to catch up on everything else. Then I was called in for a meeting with my adviser and assigned to 64 new projects that could consume every free moment of my summer but will certainly instill every wasted moment with a twinge of guilt. I am rethinking my life choices this weekend. Where am I heading? I can't even say that seriously because it's such an old familiar refrain to me. When I was complaining mildly about graduate school the last time I saw my dad, he, a man of few and infrequent words, said, "Well you have to stick to a job some day Dara!" And when my dad says something like that, you ought to take notice and read depths into it. I like grad school - I just don't like sticking. What if all I ever wanted to do was travel? And I'm heading down a tunnel of office work when I very well could have been a traveling sociologist, if I had only gotten hooked up with the right professor. And I'm damn well sick and tired of being poor.

Which is why planning my "trips" yesterday turned into a nightmare. Flights are so so expensive nowadays!! I have a family reunion in Washington state at the end of July - it will cost $600 plus two 8-13 hour trips for a weekend. I told my mother "it's not worth it" and we fought. I need to be in Boston immediately afterwards for two conferences I'm presenting at and have decided I am driving there. One of my road trips will cost as much as flying but be such a better investment and make me feel like I had a real vacation this year. Driving seems like a sin nowadays though - maybe flying is just as much of one though?

I think I mentioned that I might try online dating? So I have. To force myself to date frequently and well. And I have. They are good men - smart, wealthy and horrible. EHarmony is laden with engineers and Indians. I don't know if Indian engineers are my destiny, are a byproduct of living in Austin, or are a desperate group. I haven't actually been out with the Indians but nearly every guy has been an engineer. I ask for details on what they do and it begins with good intentions on my part and swiftly descends into "blah blah..." coming out of their mouths while I nod and smile at appropriate moments. The guy on Saturday night spent 80% of the date drawing different types of waves on napkins for me, in an attempt to explain the difference between digital and analog. And I still don't understand the difference. They all have fatal flaws as well which makes me suspect that EHarmony is for losers, and I can count myself as one now too. Saturday: A man's head on a child's body. Friday: Effeminate compounded with conversation that centered around his best male friend who just got married (no surprise that he and the wife don't get on too well). Wednesday: Shorter than my 3rd grade niece. My girl friends/sisters are chiding me for being too picky but these are the same women who disapproved of every boyfriend or date whom I was actually attracted to... Outside of all of this, it takes an abominable amount of time and is not pleasurable, e.g., I send you emails b/c I like you. So that's that.

:-) Dara

From: Andrew Marx
To: dshifrer
Subject: RE:
Date: Tue, 27 May 2008

Hello. We peaked at 80 degrees yesterday and there was a nice breeze. I actually spent a good chunk of the day outdoors. We went to the Esplanade and I washed my car (to no avail, the pollen is treacherous). It was a way better day than anticipated though I've been in a pretty bad mood the last few weeks because of work. Maybe it's just time for a vacation or, I don't know, I'm always hesitant to say my work relationship is permanently broken. Mostly because my complaints about work have been the same pretty much since I started. I have these seasonal outbreaks of work-related stress. This one I'm going through now is particularly bad. I updated my resume but there isn't a whole lot to apply for.

Despite this, the temptation to give notice is strong. I'm not claiming it's particularly rationale. I'm hoping it passes sooner or later. Real vacation begins on the 19th which is three weeks from now. A long 3 weeks, I think. (And the other thing is that there is no shortage of work; I'm overloaded as it is).

All of this is a roundabout way of sympathizing with you. I've been here for six years, mostly doing the same work. And my work is cyclical so it always comes around to bite me in the ass later.

I don't really understand your reference to road trips. Driving to/from Austin to Boston? That's quite a commitment. It always sounds good but it's tough to do when you have to be somewhere on a schedule. Someone asked me about my road trip when I moved to Boston the other day. It's not something I think about much; seems somewhat portentous except I have no desire to shake things up like that.

Finally, I have nothing to say about dating anymore. I don't like gay men usually for being pretentious but I can't believe that they're all like that so maybe I'm never looking in the right place. One of my close Boston friends tells me it will all happen in time, when I stop looking for it. Because that's exactly how it happened for him. I don't know if I believe that. If you sit in your cubicle waiting for a sign from God that this is the man you are going to marry, you better hope he's a winner.

From: Dara Shifrer
To: amarx
Subject: RE:
Date: Thu, 29 May 2008

I guess I can always count on you to sympathize with my job angst. We seem to have a similar bent toward work/life. Could you take a class to up your website tech skills? It does seem like the sort of field that requires luck or rare talent. But you I think have the   latter so I wish you could find a way to make it your central occupation. Maybe you have already fallen back into happy complacency with your current job though. ;-)

I am planning to drive from Austin to Boston. And it will take even longer than you're referencing b/c I plan to drive the scenic highways, following my road trip book guidelines. It's my only shot at a real vacation and I like driving much more than the average girl. I told my mother the other night and she literally screamed in horror. Genuine horror. It was hugely hilarious to me. The teenager in me for sure.

I have mostly decided that I will not find a life partner because of the peculiarities of my nature and it's sort of freeing b/c it's incredibly depressing to be hopeful and trying without any real means for effecting a change. Of course that sentence is ridiculous in light of my EHarmony participation, but it's more going through the motions, pleasing my critics who say that I don't try hard enough. On that topic, I almost wrote to apologize for being so nasty about my dates. It was a pretty despicable little paragraph and not a fair representation of their true worth... but right after I had decided I should send such an email to you, I got a confirmation for a date with a new one and he said he wanted to give me a heads up that he's totally blind so I wasn't completely exaggerating since that is a verifiable disability.

In better news, I just got a check for $2800 for hail damage to my car from the recent storm/tornado. And I'm going to take that money and run and pay that baby off! What a stroke of luck. My dad and I are trying to figure out if that's a wise decision, my mother just whined in horror...

:-) Dara

From: Andrew Marx
To: dshifrer
Subject: RE:
Date: Fri, 30 May 2008

I don't need an excuse to quit, I just need to make sure I can pay rent.

I'm really surprised you're driving (mostly because you have to drive back). Boston itself is really hard to navigate. There are some great restaurants. Though if you want to do something touristy whilst eating, I can find some places to choose from in the trendy areas of downtown.

I don't know if I can say anything about dating that you haven't heard before. But I will tell you that I am emphatically attracted only to straight-like guys (mostly because they aren't some variation of screaming queens) which makes dating impossible. It's almost two years to the day since I last had a boyfriend (loathsome term) and my prospects aren't great.

I hear this a lot from my friends: "I would introduce you to [insert name] but you're too aggressive/mean/forward." It's not a great thing to hear. I respond with "I can be charming, especially when I'm trying." But I've probably heard that critique from 5 friends on completely different occasions, all of whom steadfastly refuse to introduce me to a single available man. Perhaps they like me better single? There's a conspiracy in their somewhere, if I was only paranoid enough to embrace it.

I enjoy the guy downstairs, but aside from stopping in the hall to talk to him, I have no sense if he's a) available b) single c) pursuable. Online dating doesn't work for me. It requires such finesse on the part of both parties to succeed. Though my friends Jack and Josephine met online and are getting married in September, so I guess that's one success story. I'm going to his bachelor party in Vegas in a few weeks. A weekend of gambling, booze and boobs. If there is something particularly liberating about watching two women having sex with a dildo, you will be the first to know.

I think your notion of not finding a life partner strikes quite a chord with me. I have thought that way for a long time now. The only slim hope is that there are billions of people in the world, someone somewhere must be a good match. Unfortunately, where he is, I don't know. I'm not interested in random hookups and I'm not having luck with long term dating. Everyone seems to think that will change eventually so I guess we'll see how the wind blows. I wasn't ready, emotionally or otherwise, to be in a long term relationship until recently, but I think there's something to getting your feet wet, so to speak, even when you're immature. Which I didn't do much of either.

From: Dara Shifrer
To: amarx
Subject: RE:
Date: Tue, 3 Jun 2008

I am appalled on a daily basis by the noncommittal leadership of my adviser. No clear expectations but then suddenly you're in trouble because you did not interpret her vague recommendations in the way she really meant you to. She hired an undergrad to be the project assistant and is giving her to me to supervise and oh I can't wait to lay down some structure: specific hours, specific duties... How beautiful it will be!

Well my actual plan is to drive up along the Appalachian trail, playing John Denver the whole way (he references the Shenandoah Valley and the Smokey Mountains and I adore him though came to find out he was an alcoholic wife-abuser). And then I will drive back along the East coastline highway. This of course lengthens the trip dramatically. And I find myself wavering like I NEVER would have as a youth. Oh old age. But it's b/c on previous optimistic road trips I found myself quite overwhelmed with the amount of driving/time actually required and I suppose I've gotten wiser. We'll see. I don't know where I want to eat - touristy doesn't sound good but I'm not sure what kind of attractions a touristy dinner might involve. It doesn't need to be a really cheap place at all. Somewhere quiet where we can talk and the food is pretty good is fine by me. I'm glad you're so close!

I didn't realize that you were attracted to straight men - that's a curse my friend. Though it makes sense with your anathema for flamboyance. Is the one you like on the floor below the anxious pot smoking one you had dealings with a long time ago?... I'm thinking not. All the men in your life blend together, I'm afraid to say. I'm having a phone relationship (2 phone calls) with an Indian engineer named Chai in Salt Lake City. I'm attracted to his writing - he's incredibly literate. We spent the entire conversation last night talking about the non-necessity of marriage and how we can be happy on our own, which is ironic or exactly the reason why we are two 30-somethings who met on EHarmony. I think that like you, my growth has been retarded by my late start. You didn't say it in that way but that's how I interpret it for myself. If I'd made my mistakes in high school, I imagine a 20s filled with meaningful and directional relationships.

I ought to be working... as always!

Dara :-)

From: Andrew Marx
To: dshifrer
Subject: RE:
Date: Tue, 3 Jun 2008

My first job interview in years is this Thursday. Hopefully I won't be too rusty.

No, I (was) (am) a late bloomer. Now that I'm ready and mature enough for a relationship, it's harder to find quality singles. I've been a little whiny to my friends lately but I am trying to impress upon them that possibilities are endless and it's only their attitude that gets in the way (which I believe is true but somehow, my attitude gets in the way anyhow). I have a pattern of finding my next relationship about every two years (even numbered years) which would mean I was due RIGHT NOW. But none of those so-called relationships ever lasted very long so I'm not sure if I should rely on some sort of cosmic calendar to spur a new romance. Maybe this time I can make it stick...

I went for drinks tonight with some classmates. One of the guys matter of factly told us he dated his girlfriend now for 5 years (still dating) and had no intention of pursuing anything beyond "dating". To which my friend said, totally horrified "What if she *thinks* you guys are going somewhere?" (Such a girl reaction, that is).

I said to him, "Are you worried about breaking up with her and not finding someone new?"

He said, "No, I'm good looking enough."

Gotta love it. All about attitude baby.

From: Dara Shifrer
To: amarx
Subject: No, I'm good looking enough
Date: Sun, 8 Jun 2008

How'd the job interview go?

Nice of you to be convincing your friends that the possibilities are endless - that's a very positive attitude for an Andy Marx to be taking. I just can't worry about it anymore. I will be nice to people but I think a lot of it is smoke and mirrors. These deadlines - life is much longer than we think. Maybe my margarita at lunch is making me wax nonchalant about it. That's really strange because I have a two year pattern too! The unfortunate thing is that I've dabbled so much with Michael that I'm not sure when I can start counting - optimistically, I could put it at a year. Maybe YOU have already met your next relationshipee since you sent the email.

I guess it is a girl reaction because I react to that guy in the same way. That's fine to have relationships that are going nowhere as long as both people are aware... well I don't know. Then it's just not a 'relationship.' Not in the classic sense. The thing is I guarantee that guy's woman has no idea he talks that way about her. Probably of course because she would have a fit if he told her. The second thing is that he'll probably marry her despite his cockiness. Amusing story though.

So I went for drinks with my adviser and another woman I work with (an adult to me though I have friends who are her age...a superior I guess I mean). So it's come to that. I felt coerced. We have probably gotten that grant we applied for this spring so my adviser felt it was necessary to celebrate and

I could hardly say no. She must have sensed my hesitance and asked why I wasn't excited. I told her I was celebrating on the inside. And she asked if I had doubts. And I said well yes. I didn't tell her that I am very uncomfortable at the thought of being tied to her for the next three years (because of funding through the grant), that I think about leaving her on a monthly basis, etc. etc. Just that it was "big" or some nonsense, but she knows. She turned to me and cackled "Now we're married!" He he he he!!! Evil woman.

Went hiking with a sociology gal pal this morning. She's so darling I can hardly stand it. She's all of 23 but a little wise one. She's so naive and hopeful about life and the world, it's touching. Michael mocked her terribly when they met - as you might very well have ;-) - but she's a perfect person to slip into reveries with. I think I'm entering a second youth. Believing again. It gets to where being disillusioned is as much of a belief as anything...

All right, hope you're having a good weekend there.

:-) Dara

From: Andrew Marx
To: dshifrer
Subject: RE: No, I'm good looking enough.
Date: Mon, 9 Jun 2008

I was surprised with the interview. They really sold me on the job despite the fact that they didn't discuss specifics and I never talked in any specifics about myself. It was canned questions like "Tell us about a time..." I don't know what they got from that. I heard a few of the candidates dropped out because of shenanigans of one of the interviewers. I suspect they must have a second interview required but I don't know when that will be.

In the meantime, it at least sharpened my resume so that when I do find other job postings, I don't need to wait to apply for them. So that's a huge plus really. I'm really burned out at my job and my vacation is half of next week and then runs until July 1. So it's a nice time to just reassess and rejuvenate.

This month has been extra crazy. The heat isn't helping. 90 degrees plus, high humidity. Nothing is air conditioned here. I know, I sound wussy. I'm temperamental today. I got myself very wound up in May - mostly work related - and then managed to detox a bit for a while there and now I'm wound tightly again and I hate it. I don't (as a general rule) think most things in life are worth the stress but I can't seem to help myself. I'm best when I don't plan, don't try to steer my life so much. But lately, all I'm doing is trying to shove it one way or another and it's not moving fast enough for my tastes. Time has ground to a halt. It's frustrating. Not sure that made sense but it's the only way I can conceptualize it.

Alright. I guess that was the Monday ramble.

From: Dara Shifrer
To: amarx
Subject: RE: No, I'm good looking enough.
Date: Fri, 13 Jun 2008

In your interview they were doing a personality test I bet. It's the new thing or so I hear. I think it's kind of terrible - so invasive. Maybe not a personality test but they were trying to get information indirectly. Kind of lamely too - because they're only likely to trip up the really ignorant. I've heard of companies specifically giving a sit-down personality test. I'm also surprised that's not a violation of human resource law. So have you had a second interview?

No, not wussy. 90 degrees is plenty hot enough to need air conditioning. I remember driving up for family vacations in the Pacific Northwest where they advertise air conditioning at hotels like it's a bonus and being appalled. It's a sure-thing where we come from. Or at least where I came from. And certainly in Las Vegas and Austin. I think Las Vegas cooled the whole southern half of the state with their excessive air conditioning. It's miserable hot here too and I expect it will be for the next five months. I start having doubts about my love affair with Austin when the 6 month summer kicks in. Approaching or over 100 for the last three weeks. Dripping humidity. I just don't go outside... which is sad... well except for walking from my house to my bus stop and then the 15 minute hike from the bus stop to where I work on campus... which is plenty enough to dissuade me from any further going outsides.

Well my new employee is late which means I have to do her task. I am very annoyed with the whole situation. And will definitely fill you in the next time we talk.

:-) Dara

The guys are hosting a birthday party for me tonight. That's fun. I'm cooking most of it (by choice) so we're having rack of lamb, mashed potatoes and skewer vegetables. I also whipped up (literally) a shrimp dip (just shrimp, onions, olives and celery for crunch) that I'm going to top on crostinis and serve for an appetizer. The coup de grace is my cheesecake, which is world famous. I won't give China the recipe, though they're still pressing for it.

Went to a party on Saturday that was my first kegger. My first kegstand, my first beer pong and my first flip cup. My friends were like "What did you do during college?" and I was like, I don't know. I don't know. (On the flip side, I continue to be a source of amusement that never ends).

You might know, what did we do in college?

From: Dara Shifrer
To: amarx
Subject: On the flip side, I continue to be a source of amusement that never ends
Date: Wed, 27 Aug 2008

Oh, Andy! Why didn't you tell them about the time you went over to your girl friend's dorm room, played cards for about 25 minutes while taking successive slogs of vodka, mumbled that you needed to leave, walked out to the balcony and rolled over the wall, had to navigate past the door monitors guarding your building (complicated by the fact that you were their co-worker (or even supervisor?) - at least when sober), and vomited. And all before 8pm no doubt.

Well, this is all very heartening. I enjoy hearing about people in their 30s who still enjoy life. I have been feeling old and done for too long now, and I need to cut it out, because soon enough it will be true and I will have wasted all of those years when it really wasn't. Frankly, I don't know what a flip cup is. I did discover beer pong in Austin - I thought it was some strange Texas pastime but apparently Bostonians are strange too. And I have never done a kegstand in my life and don't expect to have the pleasure. Are you really 32 soon? That's so old.

I had no idea that you could cook like that or that you make globally renowned cheesecake. I'm very impressed. I still have to use a cookbook to broil potatoes or fry a steak - both of which I actually did this Saturday for my whiskey-tasting party. Yes, a whiskey-tasting party. I was simultaneously dreading and anticipating it, the latter because I have taken to liking being a host (although my damn house is so small and so hot that 15 people taxes it) and the former because people drinking whiskey seems a risky undertaking now that I'm 31. Nobody cried, fought or had sex in the backyard, so it was a success - or does that mean it was a failure? Honestly, only two people actually got tipsy and it was all by their own design. They were obnoxious. It was fun.

Well you sound like you're having a fabulous week. Oh and I almost flew to Albuquerque to meet up with my Indian boyfriend from Salt Lake City whom I have only spoke to on the phone until I cancelled it at the last minute because I was having panic attacks at night about it and hot illicit sex with Michael the other nights. Everything is under control here.

Afterword *by Andrew Marx*

A year later, I still laugh when I read this book.

It's a good thing that I think it's funny because it turned out that it is also a little more revealing than I originally intended. The events happened, mostly as described and aside from changing the names, we basically laid out a two-year period of our lives for you to laugh with us or at us.

Our goals in writing the book were as follows:

1) To make you, the reader, laugh out loud at least once when you read it
2) To talk about our passion for music without turning it into a lecture
3) To talk about the themes that Dara and I believe are central to becoming an adult, again, without turning it into a lecture
4) To tell a story that reads like a novel, regardless of our formatting choices or other editorial decisions

We did all that, and for whatever you think of the book, every decision we made was purposeful and the final product was exactly what we were aiming for.

That said, people had some problems with it.

One, the chapter out of chronological order didn't really fly with anyone else. It was done for a reason, but the question should have been: would the story have worked as well had we simply gone with a pure chronology?

Two, people thought we skimped on a few of the plot lines, leaving them hanging in the air like smoke on a humid day. One of the central themes of the book is that there are not really any concrete answers to the questions of life. So if a plot point wasn't resolved by the end, it seemed to be in keeping with the theme. Plus, frankly, life meanders on. Some things just didn't get resolved before the end of the book. But it was intended to be read as a novel, so okay, usually novels tie up loose ends.

Three, people discovered (as I did myself) a few egregious editorial mistakes that slipped by us.

So we thought it would be a good idea to address these concerns, and publish it again with new material, an expanded edition if you will, with fewer mistakes. All along, our goal was to produce the best possible story and if you're distracted by weird punctuation, angry at dangling plot points, and startled by ambiguous jumps in chronology, then the least we can do is try to fix it.

Expanded or not, our goals haven't changed. You will laugh. That's an order!

August 13, 2009

An Interview with
Andrew Marx and Dara Shifrer,
Authors of *What Do You Say to the DJ?*

Just before the release of their book What Do You Say to the DJ?,
I put the question to co-authors Andrew Marx and Dara Shifrer
that I expect everyone will be asking them sooner or later.

"An autobiography? Really? It is ever too personal?"

Marx, with a penetrating look that I will come to recognize as
one of his trademarks, tells me, "There are one or two points in
the book where I thought to myself, 'this is almost too personal'."
But he points out, it didn't stop them from writing it.

"We didn't start out thinking, 'Which genre can we tackle today?' The process was more organic than that. We wanted to tell
our stories and we thought we had a good message to share. The
core of the book is the idea that you are not alone. A lot of people
are dealing with the exact same issues you are."

The issues, such as the "long-termity" of relationships (or as it
turns out, the lack of long-termity) is a thread that twines its
way through the book. But both authors are quick to say that
although romance gets top billing, there is more powering the
book than just love and broken hearts.

Shifrer says the inspiration came from a spectrum of issues, not just one thing in particular. "I was with some friends and high school came up. And this tall, gangly, awkward but hellishly funny guy who was a radio-television-film major but now works as a pedi-cab cycler says 'I hated high school...well, I've hated it all.' And I totally knew what he meant, in each of life's new phases there are these expectations that, for some people, just don't seem to quite fit. And so our book isn't even so much about adult life because everyone has been chafed along the way."

Marx and Shifrer met in college at the University of Nevada, Las Vegas. They lived one floor apart in Tonopah Hall and fell into the same social circle. Eventually, their writing interests coincided with the publication of the literary magazine, Suedomsa the Magazine, which they published during their junior and senior years. It achieved a certain amount of local renown for them. They were featured in a Las Vegas newspaper article about literary magazines that had longevity.

Though Suedomsa was shelved when they graduated, the two stayed close. Shifrer pursued teaching and Marx began a career in higher education administration. In the ensuing years, she relocated to Austin, TX and found herself home. He drove across the country and made his home in Boston, MA. The separation of 2,000 miles hardly dented their friendship. They stayed in close contact through e-mail, which suited their nature as writers and unexpectedly laid the foundation for the book.

The local element has a shining role in their stories. There is a funny passage where Marx describes New England culture and the "traditional values on display" to which Shifrer replies, "You made it sound really unappealing to me." But that is how it goes. The affection each author has for their own city is unmistakable. It becomes a nice counterbalance to some of the heavy-handed issues that play a prominent role in the book.

What Do You Say to the DJ? taps into a lot of "coming of age" anxiety that builds around work, family, school, and of course, dating. Humor becomes a way of coping with the stress of adulthood. Music, too. Marx and Shifrer have been collaboratively building a website of live concert reviews for several years. Concert-central.com sports some 700 plus reviews, of which they have written ninety percent of them, covering almost 600 different bands and artists in the process. The book includes a number of reprinted reviews directly from the site, and part of the story is about the creation of the website.

"Music is such a driving force," Marx says, "that it would be a disservice to write a book about our lives and not talk about it to some degree."

Their respective musical knowledge is the result of a genuine long-time passion for music and dedication to bands. Their divergent tastes in music not only add to the richness of the book for real music fans, but also offer another layer of insight into their friendship. While Shifrer raves about O'Death, Of Montreal, and The Mountain Goats, Marx remains devoted to Siouxsie Sioux, Andy Bell and Johnette Napolitano.

"There is no doubt that friendship is part of the story," Shifrer says, "but that was the pleasant surprise for me. I started reading [the first draft] thinking life, work, music, etc. and ended with this realization that a major point was that the writers were actually very good friends.

"That's what good books do - lead you along, lead you along, and all along weaving in a message or theme that isn't fully realized until the end. Framing it as a friendship book or a music book not only ruins that surprise, it lays all of our cards out there."

The authors are self-publishing on the BookSurge imprint. That means the books are available on amazon.com, but not in stores. Marx said the decision came easily. "You could buy it from us directly, but otherwise, it's only available online." He explains, "The book industry suffers from high costs and a saturation of books. So most published authors get a very tiny share of the market in physical stores. We can focus our marketing efforts and still reach a wide audience by selling the book on the internet."

In the early stages of publication, they batted around ideas for promoting the book and establishing a viral presence on the web. They pushed the book on Facebook and MySpace, and even created a comic strip "interview" published on their website. "We went so far as to talk about a contest 'win a dinner with the authors,'" Marx joked, "but it's a fine line between a publicity tie-in and a dating service."

Though print-on-demand has made self-publishing relatively easy for new writers (the books are not printed until they are ordered by the customer,) there are a lot of technical details that become their responsibilities. Marx points to the back cover copy for example. "If you don't know how to write effective cover copy, you better learn fast. But I liked the idea of being involved in every stage of the process and self-publishing made sense in that respect."

The authors say family and friends have been supportive of their efforts, even those that think they might be mentioned in the book. The authors were careful to consider others' feelings, but in the end they felt the fact that it was autobiographical was a non-issue.

"The stories themselves happened," Marx says, "The e-mails, however, are not straight out of our inboxes. And we did not use real names. It's not about that."

"Meaning," Dara says, "the stirring-up-of-scandal amongst our friends and family was not an angle that was interesting to us."

The end result is a book that is damn funny, and strikes right to the heart of being a twenty-something adult. When you finish the book, you just might agree that some of it borders on too personal. But you will glad they found the courage to tell this particular tale.

January 20, 2009

Made in the USA